Printed in the United States of America

AUG   2015

Table of Contents

Introduction

Congratulations on continuing your education as you continue to prepare for becoming an educator! Before we get into the test content, we're sure you have questions – everybody does. "How hard is the exam?" "Can I pass on my first try?" "What if I don't? Can I take it again?" "What is even *on* the test?"

Don't worry! We have the answers to all of these questions and more.

While the exam isn't easy, proper planning and preparation can help ensure your success. Sure, you can take the exam again if you fail; but our goal is to give you the keys to outsmarting the exam – the first time around. These first few pages will detail everything you'll need to know about the exam, before leading you into the review material. So get ready to take some notes. Pace yourself. And above all, remember that you are taking the right first step in furthering your career.

Registering for the Exam

This can be done via telephone or computer.

> **By Phone**: Phone registration is only available in "emergency" situations, and is not applicable for "regular" or "late" registrations. Regular and Late registrations must be done by computer.

> **By Computer**: Available 24 hours a day and 7 days a week, simply visit www.in.nesinc.com and find your way to "internet registration" tab. Please note that registrations must be completed by 5:00pm to count for that day. Follow the step-by-step instructions to register, make necessary payment, and confirmation of your registration.

Testing Fees

Even if no additional fees are assessed, knowing that you'll be paying a lot your hard-earned money is an additional incentive to do your best on the exam. Re-taking the test will require you to pay the same fees again – not properly preparing can have expensive consequences!

- The test fee is $38 per subtest, but please note that test centers may at their discretion charge additional fees, so you must check beforehand!

What's on the Exam

The content of the question will follow the below categories

- **<u>Reading Comprehension</u>**
- **<u>Language Arts</u>**
- **<u>Mathematics</u>**

How is the Exam Scored?

You will be scored on a range of 100 to 300 points, with a passing score being 220 or greater.

Test Day

Identification Policy: You must bring to the test administration a current, government-issued identification printed in English, in the name in which you registered, bearing your photograph and signature. Copies will not be accepted.

Acceptable forms of government-issued identification include the following:

- Driver's license with photograph and signature
- Passport with photograph and signature
- State identification with photograph and signature (provided by the Department of Licensing for individuals who do not have a driver's license)
- National identification with photograph and signature
- Military identification with photograph and signature
- Alien Registration Card (green card, permanent resident visa)

Unacceptable forms of identification:

- draft classification cards
- credit cards of any kind
- social security cards, student IDs
- international driver's licenses
- international student IDs
- notary-prepared letters or documents
- employee identification cards
- learner's permits or any temporary identification cards
- automated teller machine (ATM) cards

If you do not have proper identification at the time of your test, you will be denied admission to the test session. If you are refused admission to the test for any reason, you will be considered absent and will receive no credit or refund of any kind.

If the name on your identification differs from the name in which you are registered, you must bring **official, original** verification of the change (e.g., original marriage certificate, original court order).

If you have any questions about your identification, call Evaluation Systems at (916) 928-4192 or (800) 784-4999 before the day of the test.

You MUST Bring

As you head to the testing center, don't forget to bring your ID and any necessary documentation, as well as your Admission Ticket.

You May NOT Bring

Basically, if it's not your Admission Ticket, ID, or any approved device, you can't have it with you. Specifically, you can't bring these items into the testing room:

1. Cell phones, smartphones, or PDAs.
2. Any electronic recording, photographic, or listening device.
3. Food, drink, or tobacco products.
4. Personal items (purses, backpacks, etc.).
5. Paper, pencils, notes, reference material, etc.
6. Weapons of any type.

As if those precautions were not enough, you can also expect to be fingerprinted and/or photographed after entering the testing facility. You may be asked to undergo a quick scan from a metal detecting device before being allowed into the testing room. Additionally, you may be asked to sign a waiver stating that you understand the test administration will be videotaped.

In the event that you object to any of these security measures, you will not be allowed to test.

After the Test

Your test scores will be reported to you, as well as the institution(s) listed when you registered. Check your "test dates" calendar online to see when score reports will be available.

Scores are sometimes delayed if there is a problem with the processing or if there is a new computer test being administered. In addition, your scores will be delayed if there are problems with your payment, and your scores may be permanently voided if you have any outstanding balance owed by you to Evaluation Systems after a test administration for which you were registered.

Unofficial Test Results at a Computer-Based Test Center

At the end of your test, you'll get an "unofficial score". Keep in mind that these scores are not valid for reporting as an official score. You will get your official recorded score at a later date that is valid for use in official capacities.

Chapter 1: Mathematics

The CASA Math section will test your knowledge of the following concepts:

- **Numbers and Operations**

- **Algebra**

- **Geometry**

- **Data Analysis**

- **Statistics**

- **Probability**

We'll provide an extensive review of these subjects, as well as giving you the chance to run some practice drills. However, this section is NOT designed to TEACH you math; the CASA covers math concepts learned through the tenth grade, which means you don't need to learn any new information. In fact, you don't need to worry at all about working with endless, bulky calculations; writing geometry proofs; working with imaginary numbers; Calculus; or Trigonometry – none of them are covered on the CASA.

No Calculators

Don't rely on a calculator while you practice, because you aren't allowed to use one during the test! Just like in sports, you need to practice how you want to play, so cheating now while you practice would be a disservice to yourself.

The Most Common Mistakes

People make mistakes all the time – but during a test, those mistakes can make the difference between an excellent score, or one which falls below the requirements. Watch out for these common mistakes that people make on the CASA:

- Answering with the wrong sign (positive / negative).

- Mixing up the Order of Operations.

- Misplacing a decimal.

- Not reading the question thoroughly (and therefore providing an answer that was not asked for.)

- Circling the wrong letter, or filling in wrong circle choice.

If you're thinking, "Those are just common sense" – exactly! Most of the mistakes made on the CASA are simple mistakes. Regardless, they still result in a wrong answer and the loss of a potential point.

Strategies for the Mathematics Section

1. **Go Back to the Basics**: First and foremost, practice your basic skills: sign changes, order of operations, simplifying fractions, and equation manipulation. These are the skills used most on the CASA, though they are applied in different contexts. Remember that when it comes right down to it, all math problems rely on the four basic skills of addition, subtraction, multiplication, and division. All that changes is the order in which they are used to solve a problem.

2. **Don't Rely on Mental Math**: Using mental math is great for eliminating answer choices, but ALWAYS WRITE IT DOWN! This cannot be stressed enough. Use whatever paper is provided; by writing and/or drawing out the problem, you are more likely to catch any mistakes. The act of writing things down forces you to organize your calculations, leading to an improvement in your CASA score.

3. **The Three-Times Rule**:

   - **Step One – Read the question**: Write out the given information.

   - **Step Two – Read the question**: Set up your equation(s) and solve.

   - **Step Three – Read the question**: Make sure that your answer makes sense (is the amount too large or small, is the answer in the correct unit of measure, etc.).

4. **Make an Educated Guess**: Eliminate those answer choices which you are relatively sure are incorrect, and then guess from the remaining choices. Educated guessing is critical to increasing your score.

Math Concepts Tested on the CASA

You need to practice in order to score well on the test. To make the most out of your practice, use this guide to determine the areas for which you need more review. Most importantly, practice all areas under testing circumstances (a quiet area, a timed practice test, no looking up facts as you practice, etc.)

When reviewing, take your time and let your brain recall the necessary math. If you are taking the CASA, then you have already had course instruction in these areas. The examples given will "jog" your memory.

The next few pages will cover various math subjects (starting with the basics, but in no particular order), along with worked examples.

CASA Formulas and Facts (Given)

You might see the formulas provided, but you should still review them now, since they will not be given with descriptions or examples.

1. **Diameter of a Circle** = 2 * Radius (r).

2. **Circumference of a Circle** = 2 * Radius (r) * π.

3. **Area of a Circle** = π * Radius (r)^2.

4. **Area of a Rectangle** = Length (l) * Width (w).

5. **Area of a Triangle** = ½ * Base (b) * Height (h).

6. **Volume of a Cube** = Length (l) * Width (w) * Height (h).

7. **Volume of a Cylinder** = Height (h) * Radius (r)^2 * π.

8. **The Pythagorean Theorem** (Finding Diagonal Length): Length of the Diagonal (c)^2 = Sum of the Two Remaining Squared Sides ($a^2 + b^2$).

9. **Surface Area of a Sphere** = 4 * Radius (r)^2 * π.

10. **Volume of a Sphere** = $^4/_3$ * Radius (r)^3 * π.

11. **Number of Degrees of an Arc in a Circle** = 360°

12. **Measure of Degrees of a Straight Angle** = 180°.

13. **Sum of Degrees of the Angles in a Triangle** = 180°.

The next few pages will cover those formulas and facts which will not be given to you before the test. Review them thoroughly, and take advantage of the "Test Your Knowledge" sections that we've provided – practice makes perfect!

Formulas and Facts (NOT Given)

Positive & Negative Number Rules

(+) + (-) = Subtract the two numbers. Solution gets the sign of the larger number.

(-) + (-) = Negative number.

(-) * (-) = Positive number.

(-) * (+) = Negative number.

(-) / (-) = Positive number.

(-) / (+) = Negative number.

Order of Operations

PEMDAS – **P**arentheses/**E**xponents/**M**ultiply/**D**ivide/**A**dd/**S**ubtract

Perform the operations within parentheses first, and then any exponents. After those steps, perform all multiplication and division. (These are done from left to right, as they appear in the problem) Finally, do all required addition and subtraction, also from left to right as they appear in the problem.

Examples:

1. Solve $(-(2)^2 - (4 + 7))$:
   - $(-4 - 11) = -15$.

2. Solve $((5)^2 \div 5 + 4 * 2)$:
   - $25 \div 5 + 4 * 2$.
   - $5 + 8 = 13$.

Greatest Common Factor (GCF)

The greatest factor that divides two numbers.

Example: The GCF of 24 and 18 is 6. 6 is the largest number, or greatest factor, that can divide both 24 and 18.

Probabilities

A probability is found by dividing the number of desired outcomes by the number of possible outcomes. (The piece divided by the whole.)

Example: What is the probability of picking a blue marble if 3 of the 15 marbles are blue?

$3/15 = 1/5$. The probability is **1 in 5** that a blue marble is picked.

Fractions

Adding and subtracting fractions requires a common denominator

Find a common denominator for:

$$\frac{2}{3} - \frac{1}{5}.$$

$$\frac{2}{3} - \frac{1}{5} = \frac{2}{3}\left(\frac{5}{5}\right) - \frac{1}{5}\left(\frac{3}{3}\right) \quad = \quad \frac{10}{15} - \frac{3}{15} = \mathbf{\frac{7}{15}}.$$

To add mixed fractions, work first the whole numbers, and then the fractions.

$$2\frac{1}{4} + 1\frac{3}{4} = 3\frac{4}{4} = \mathbf{4}.$$

To subtract mixed fractions, convert to single fractions by multiplying the whole number by the denominator and adding the numerator. Then work as above.

$$2\frac{1}{4} - 1\frac{3}{4} = \frac{9}{4} - \frac{7}{4} = \frac{2}{4} = \mathbf{\frac{1}{2}}.$$

To multiply fractions, convert any mixed fractions into single fractions and multiply across; reduce to lowest terms if needed.

$$2\frac{1}{4} * 1\frac{3}{4} = \frac{9}{4} * \frac{7}{4} = \frac{63}{16} = \mathbf{3\frac{15}{16}}.$$

To divide fractions, convert any mixed fractions into single fractions, flip the second fraction, and then multiply across.

$$2\frac{1}{4} \div 1\frac{3}{4} = \frac{9}{4} \div \frac{7}{4} = \frac{9}{4} * \frac{4}{7} = \frac{36}{28} = 1\frac{8}{28} = \mathbf{1\frac{2}{7}}.$$

Simple Interest

Interest * Principle.

> **Example:** If I deposit $500 into an account with an annual rate of 5%, how much will I have after 2 years?

1st year: $500 + (500*.05) = 525$.

2nd year: $525 + (525*.05) = \mathbf{551.25}$.

Prime Factorization

Expand to prime number factors.

> **Example:** $104 = 2 * 2 * 2 * 13$.

Absolute Value

The absolute value of a number is its distance from zero, not its value.

So in $|x| = a$, "x" will equal "$-a$" as well as "a."

Likewise, $|3| = 3$, and $|-3| = 3$.

Equations with absolute values will have two answers. Solve each absolute value possibility separately. All solutions must be checked into the original equation.

> **Example:** Solve for x: $|2x - 3| = x + 1$
>
> 1. Equation One: $2x - 3 = -(x + 1)$.
>   - $2x - 3 = -x - 1$.
>   - $3x = 2$.
>   - $x = 2/3$.
>
> 2. Equation Two: $2x - 3 = x + 1$.
>   - $x = 4$.

Mean, Median, Mode

Mean is a math term for "average." Total all terms and divide by the number of terms.

> Find the mean of 24, 27, and 18.
>
> $24 + 27 + 18 = 69 \div 3 = \textbf{23}$.

Median is the middle number of a given set, found after the numbers have all been put in numerical order. In the case of a set of even numbers, the middle two numbers are averaged.

> What is the median of 24, 27, and 18?
>
> 18, **24**, 27.
>
> What is the median of 24, 27, 18, and 19?
>
> 18, 19, 24, 27 ($19 + 24 = 43$. $43/2 = \textbf{21.5}$).

Mode is the number which occurs most frequently within a given set.

> What is the mode of 2, 5, 4, 4, 3, 2, 8, 9, 2, 7, 2, and 2?
>
> The mode would be **2** because it appears the most within the set.

Combined Average

Weigh each average individual average before determining the sum.

> **Example**: If Cory averaged 3 hits per game during the summer and 2 hits per game during the fall and played 7 games in the summer and 8 games in the fall, what was his hit average overall?
>
> 1. Weigh each average.
>   - Summer: 3 * 7 = 21.
>   - Fall: 2 * 8 = 16.
>   - Sum: 21 + 16 = 47.
>
> 2. Total number of games: 7 + 8 = 15.
>
> 3. Calculate average: 47/15 = ~ **3.13 hits/game**.

You may need to work a combined average problem with a missing term.

> **Example**: Bobbie paid an average of $20 a piece for ten shirts. If five of the shirts averaged $15 each, what was the average cost of the remaining shirts?
>
> 1. Calculate sum: 10 * 20 = 200.
>
> 2. Calculate sub-sum #1: 5 *15 = 75.
>
> 3. Calculate sub-sum #2: 200 – 75 = 125.
>
> 4. Calculate average: 125 / 5 = **$25**.

Percent, Part, & Whole

Part = Percent * Whole.

Percent = Part / Whole.

Whole = Part / Percent.

> **Example:** Jim spent 30% of his paycheck at the fair. He spent $15 for a hat, $30 for a shirt, and $20 playing games. How much was his check? (Round to nearest dollar.)
>
> Whole = 65 / .30 = **$217.00**.

Percent Change

Percent Change = Amount of Change / Original Amount * 100.

Percent Increase = (New Amount – Original Amount) / Original Amount * 100.

Percent Decrease = (Original Amount – New Amount) / Original Amount * 100.

Amount Increase (or **Decrease**) = Original Price * Percent Markup (or Markdown).

Original Price = New Price / (Whole - Percent Markdown [or Markup]).

> **Example:** A car that was originally priced at $8300 has been reduced to $6995. What percent has it been reduced?
>
> (8300 – 6995) / 8300 * 100 = **15.72%**.

Repeated Percent Change

Increase: Final amount = Original Amount * $(1 + \text{rate})^{\text{\# of changes}}$.

Decrease: Final Amount = Original Amount * $(1 - \text{rate})^{\text{\# of changes}}$.

> **Example:** The weight of a tube of toothpaste decreases by 3% each time it is used. If it weighed 76.5 grams when new, what is its weight in grams after 15 uses?
>
> Final amount = $76.5 * (1 - .3)^{15}$.
>
> $76.5 * (.97)^{15}$ = **48.44 grams**.

Ratios

To solve a ratio, simply find the equivalent fraction. To distribute a whole across a ratio:

1. Total all parts.

2. Divide the whole by the total number of parts.

3. Multiply quotient by corresponding part of ratio.

> **Example:** There are 90 voters in a room, and they are either Democrat or Republican. The ratio of Democrats to Republicans is 5:4. How many Republicans are there?
>
> 1. 5 + 4 = 9.
>
> 2. 90 / 9 = 10.
>
> 3. 10 * 4 = **40 Republicans**.

Proportions

Direct Proportions: Corresponding ratio parts change in the same direction (increase/decrease).

Indirect Proportions: Corresponding ratio parts change in opposite directions (as one part increases the other decreases).

Example: A train traveling 120 miles takes 3 hours to get to its destination. How long will it take if the train travels 180 miles?

120 mph:180 mph is to x hours:3 hours. (Write as fraction and cross multiply.)
- $120/3 = 180/x$.
- $540 = 120x$.
- $x = \textbf{4.5 hours}$.

Arithmetic Sequence

Each term is equal to the previous term plus x.

Example: 2, 5, 8, 11.
- $2 + 3 = 5$; $5 + 3 = 8$ … etc.
- $x = \textbf{3}$.

Geometric Sequence

Each term is equal to the previous term multiplied by x.

Example: 2, 4, 8, 16.
- $x = \textbf{2}$.

Roots

Root of a Product: $\sqrt[n]{a \cdot b} = \sqrt[n]{a} \cdot \sqrt[n]{b}$.

Root of a Quotient: $\sqrt[n]{\dfrac{a}{b}} = \dfrac{\sqrt[n]{a}}{\sqrt[n]{b}}$.

Fractional Exponent: $\sqrt[n]{a^{m}} = a^{m/n}$.

Literal Equations

Equations with more than one variable. Solve in terms of one variable first.

Example: Solve for y: $4x + 3y = 3x + 2y$.

1. Combine like terms: $3y - 2y = 4x - 2x$.

2. Solve for y. $y = \textbf{-x}$.

Linear Systems

A linear system requires the solving of two literal equations simultaneously. There are two different methods (Substitution and Addition) that can be used to solve linear systems.

Substitution Method: Solve for one variable first, and then substitute.

 Example: Solve for x and y: $3y - 4 + x = 0$ and $5x + 6y = 11$.

1. Solve for one variable.
   - $3y - 4 + x = 0$.
   - $3y + x = 4$.
   - $x = 4 - 3y$.

2. Substitute into second equation, and solve.
   - $5(4 - 3y) + 6y = 11$.
   - $20 - 15y + 6y = 11$.
   - $20 - 9y = 11$.
   - $-9y = -9$.
   - $y = 1$.

3. Substitute into first equation.
   - $3(1) - 4 + x = 0$.
   - $-1 + x = 0$.
   - $x = 1$.

Addition Method: Manipulate one of the equations so that when added to the other, one variable is eliminated.

 Example: Solve $2x + 4y = 8$ and $4x + 2y = 10$.

1. Manipulate one equation to eliminate a variable when added together.
   - $-2(2x + 4y = 8) = (-4x - 8y = -16)$.
   - $(-4x - 8y = -16) + (4x + 2y = 10)$.
   - $-6y = -6$.
   - $y = 1$.

2. Plug into an equation and solve for the other variable.
   - $2x + 4(1) = 8$.
   - $2x + 4 = 8$.
   - $2x = 4$.
   - $x = 2$.

The following is a typical word problem that would use a linear system to solve.

Example: Tommy has a collection of coins worth $5.20. He has 8 more nickels than quarters. How many of each does he have?

1. Set up equations.
    - Let n = nickels and q = quarters.
    - $.05n + .25q = 5.2$.
    - $n = q + 8$.

2. Substitute Equation 2 into Equation 1.
    - $.05(q + 8) + .25q = 5.2$.

3. Solve for q. You can ignore the decimal point and negative sign after this step because you are solving for number of coins.
    - $-.05(q + 8) + .25q = 5.2$.
    - $.05q + .4 + .25q = 5.2$.
    - $q = 16$.

4. Plug into the original equation.
    - $n = q + 8$.
    - $n = 24$.
    - $q = 16$.

Linear Equations

An equation for a straight line. The variable CANNOT have an exponent, square roots, cube roots, etc.

Example: $y = 2x + 1$ is a straight line, with "1" being the y-intercept, and "2" being the positive slope.

Algebraic Equations

When simplifying or solving algebraic equations, you need to be able to utilize all math rules: exponents, roots, negatives, order of operations, etc.

1. Add & Subtract: Only the coefficients of like terms.

    Example: $5xy + 7y + 2yz + 11xy - 5yz = 16xy + 7y - 3yz$.

2. Multiplication: First the coefficients then the variables.

    Example: Monomial * Monomial. (Remember: a variable with no exponent has an implied exponent of 1.)
    - $(3x^4y^2z)(2y^4z^5) = 6x^4y^6z^6$.

    Example: Monomial * Polynomial.
    - $(2y^2)(y^3 + 2xy^2z + 4z) = 2y^5 + 4xy^4z + 8y^2z$

Example: Binomial * Binomial.

- $(5x + 2)(3x + 3)$. Remember: FOIL (First, Outer, Inner, Last).

  First: $5x * 3x = 15x^2$.

  Outer: $5x * 3 = 15x$.

  Inner: $2 * 3x = 6x$.

  Last: $2 * 3 = 6$.

  Combine like terms: $15x^2 + 21x + 6$.

Example: Binomial * Polynomial.

- $(x + 3)(2x^2 - 5x - 2)$.

  First Term: $x(2x^2 - 5x - 2) = 2x^3 - 5x^2 - 2x$.

  Second term: $3(2x^2 - 5x - 2) = 6x^2 - 15x - 6$.

  Added Together: $2x^3 + x^2 - 17x - 6$.

Inequalities

Inequalities are solved like linear and algebraic equations, except the sign must be reversed when dividing by a negative number.

Example: $-7x + 2 < 6 - 5x$.

Step 1 – Combine like terms: $-2x < 4$.

Step 2 – Solve for x. (Reverse the sign): $x > -2$.

Solving compound inequalities will give you two answers.

Example: $-4 \leq 2x - 2 \leq 6$.

Step 1 – Add 2 to each term to isolate x: $-2 \leq 2x \leq 8$.

Step 2: Divide by 2: $-1 \leq x \leq 4$.

Solution set is **[-1, 4]**.

Exponent Rules

Rule	Example
$x^0 = 1$	$5^0 = 1$
$x^1 - x$	$5^1 = 5$
$x^a \cdot x^b = x^{a+b}$	$5^2 * 5^3 = 5^5$
$(xy)^a = x^a y^a$	$(5 * 6)^2 = 5^2 * 6^2 = 25 *36$
$(x^a)^b = x^{ab}$	$(5^2)^3 = 5^6$
$(x/y)^a = x^a/y^a$	$(10/5)^2 = 10^2/5^2 = 100/25$
$x^a/y^b = x^{a-b}$	$5^4/5^3 = 5^1 = 5$ (remember $x \neq 0$)
$x^{1/a} = \sqrt[a]{x}$	$25^{1/2} = \sqrt[2]{25} = 5$
$x^{-a} = \dfrac{1}{x^a}$	$5^{-2} = \dfrac{1}{5^2} = \dfrac{1}{25}$ (remember $x \neq 0$)
$(-x)^a$ = positive number if "a" is even; negative number if "a" is odd.	

Slope

The formula used to calculate the slope (m) of a straight line connecting two points is: $m = (y_2 - y_1) / (x_2 - x_1)$ = change in y / change in x.

Example: Calculate slope of the line in the diagram.

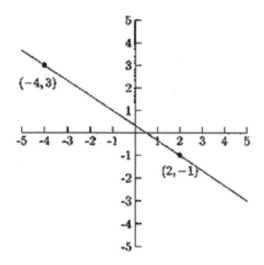

$m = (3 - (-1))/(-4 - 2) = 4/-6 = $ **- 2/3**.

Midpoint

To determine the midpoint between two points, simply add the two x coordinates together and divide by 2 (midpoint x). Then add the y coordinates together and divide by 2 (midpoint y).

$$\left(\frac{x_1 + x_2}{2}, \frac{y_1 + y}{2} \right)$$

Fundamental Counting Principle

(The number of possibilities of an event happening) * (the number of possibilities of another event happening) = the total number of possibilities.

> **Example**: If you take a multiple choice test with 5 questions, with 4 answer choices for each question, how many test result possibilities are there?

> **Solution**: Question 1 has 4 choices; question 2 has 4 choices; etc.

4 *4 * 4 * 4 * 4 (one for each question) = **1024 possible test results**.

Permutations

> The number of ways a set number of items can be arranged. Recognized by the use of a factorial ($n!$), with n being the number of items.

> If $n = 3$, then $3! = 3 * 2 * 1 = 6$. If you need to arrange n number of things but x number are alike, then $n!$ is divided by $x!$

> > **Example**: How many different ways can the letters in the word **balance** be arranged?

> > **Solution**: There are 7 letters, so $n! = 7!$ But 2 letters are the same, so $x! = 2!$ Set up the equation:
> > $$\frac{7 * 6 * 5 * 4 * 3 * 2 * 1}{2 * 1} = \textbf{2540 ways}.$$

Combinations

> To calculate total number of possible combinations, use the formula: $n!/r! \ (n-r)!$
> Where n = # of objects; and r = # of objects selected at a time.

> > **Example**: If seven people are selected in groups of three, how many different combinations are possible?

> > **Solution**:
> > $$\frac{7 * 6 * 5 * 4 * 3 * 2 * 1}{(3 * 2 * 1)(7-3)} = \textbf{210 possible combinations}.$$

Functions and Their Rules

Functions are simple if you think of them as just another substitution problem. Pay attention to your math, always double check your signs, and check your answer.

Function	Rule	Example
Adding	$(f + g)(x) = f(x) + g(x)$.	If $f(x) = 3x + 2$ and $g(x) = x^2$, then $(f + g)(x) = 3x + 2 + x^2$.
Subtracting	$(f - g)(x) = f(x) - g(x)$.	If $f(x) = 3x + 2$ and $g(x) = x^2$, then $(f - g)(x) = 3x + 2 - x^2$.
Multiplying	$(f * g)(x) = f(x) * g(x)$.	If $f(x) = 3x + 2$ and $g(x) = x^2$, then $(f * g)(x) = (3x + 2) * x^2$.
Dividing	$(f / g)(x) = f(x) / g(x)$, provided $g(x) \neq 0$.	If $f(x) = 3x + 2$ and $g(x) = x^2$, then $(f / g)(x) = (3x + 2) / x^2$.
Composition	$(f \circ g)(x) = f(g(x))$. [Replace each x in the formula of $f(x)$ with the entire formula of $g(x)$.]	If $f(x) = x^2 - x$ and $g(x) = x - 4$, then: $(f \circ g)(x) = f(g(x))$ $= f(x - 4)$ $= (x - 4)^2 - (x - 4)$. (Can be reduced further.) $\quad$ $(g \circ f)(x) = g(f(x))$ $= g(x^2 - x)$ $= (x^2 - x) - 4$. (Can be reduced further.)
Inverse	$f^{-1}(x)$ = the inverse of (x); denoted by $f(f^{-1}(x)) = f^{-1}(f(x)) = x$.	If two functions, $f(x)$ and $g(x)$, are defined so that $(f \circ g)(x) = x$ and $(g \circ f)(x) = x$, then $f(x)$ and $g(x)$ are inverse functions of each other.

Strategies for Inverse Functions

To find the correct inverse function of $f(x)$ every time, you can use this procedure:

Given the function $f(x)$, we want to find the inverse function, f-1(x).

1. First, replace $f(x)$ with y. This is done to make the rest of the process easier.

2. Replace every x with a y and replace every y with an x.

3. Solve the equation from Step 2 for y. This is the step where mistakes are most often made so be careful with this step.

4. Replace y with f-1(x). In other words, we've managed to find the inverse at this point.

Example: If $f(x) = \frac{x-1}{x+1}$, find $f^{-1}(x)$.

1. $y = \frac{x-1}{x+1}$

2. $x = \frac{y-1}{y+1}$

3. $xy + x = y - 1$
   $xy - y = -x - 1$
   $y(x - 1) = -(x + 1)$
   $y = \frac{-(x+1)}{(x-1)}$

4. $f^{-1}(x) = \frac{-(x+1)}{(x-1)}$

The following is an example of a typical function problem, followed by function rules and definitions you need to know.

If $f(x) = x^2 + 3x$, find $f(x + 2)$.

1. Simply replace $(x + 2)$ for x in the first equation $(x^2 + 3x)$.
   - $(x + 2)^2 + 3(x + 2)$.

2. Use FOIL for first term.
   - $x^2 + 4x + 4 + 3x + 6$.

3. Combine like terms: $x^2 + 7x + 10$.

4. Factor: $(x + 5)(x + 2)$.

5. Set equations to zero. Solve.
   - $x + 5 = 0; x = -5$.
   - $x + 2 = 0; x = -2$.

Quadratics

Factoring: converting $ax^2 + bx + c$ to factored form. Find two numbers that are factors of c and whose sum is b.

Example: Factor $2x^2 + 12x + 18 = 0$.

1. If possible, factor out a common monomial:$2(x^2 - 6x + 9)$.

2. Find two numbers that are factors of 9; and also sum to -6: $2(x - \_)(x - \_)$.

3. Fill in the binomials. Be sure to check your answer and signs: $2(x - 3)(x - 3)$.

4. To solve, set each to $= 0$: $x - 3 = 0; x = 3$.

25

If the equation cannot be factored (there are no two factors of c that sum to $= b$), the quadratic formula is used.

$$x = \frac{-b \pm \sqrt{b^2 - 4ac}}{2a}$$

Using the same equation from the above example: $a = 2$, $b = 12$, and $c = 18$. Plug into the formula and solve. Remember there will still be two answers due to the (+) and (-) before the radical.

Graphing

You must be familiar with all the various aspects of graphing functions and quadratics, especially the following concepts:

Vertex: The turning point; can be the minimum or the maximum.
Has the coordinates (h, k). The vertex form of the quadratic equation is:

$$f(x) = a(x - h)^2 + k. \quad [\text{The vertex is at } (h, k).]$$

The formula $(\frac{-b}{2a}, f(\frac{-b}{2a}))$ (correspond with the quadratic equation) can be used to find the vertex.

Axis of Symmetry: The line that runs through the vertex. The formula used is the same as finding for h above: $h = \frac{-b}{2a}$.

Roots, Zeros, and Solutions: All the values of x which make the equation equal to zero, also known as x-intercepts.

Domain: All the possible x values of a function.

Range: All the possible output values ($f(x)$ or y values) of the function.
Translations: Translations follow these rules:

- $f(x) + k$ is $f(x)$ shifted upward k units.
- $f(x) - k$ is $f(x)$ shifted downward k units.
- $f(x + h)$ is $f(x)$ shifted left h units.
- $f(x - h)$ is $f(x)$ shifted right h units.
- $-f(x)$ is $f(x)$ flipped upside down ("reflected about the x-axis").
- $f(-x)$ is the mirror of $f(x)$ ("reflected about the y-axis").
- The graph of $y = f(x - h) + k$ is the translation of the graph – d $y = f(x)$ – by (h, k) units in the plane.

Geometry

- **Acute Angle**: Measures less than 90°.

- **Acute Triangle**: Each angle measures less than 90°.

- **Obtuse Angle**: Measures greater than 90°.

- **Obtuse Triangle**: One angle measures greater than 90°.

- **Adjacent Angles**: Share a side and a vertex.

- **Complementary Angles**: Adjacent angles that sum to 90°.

- **Supplementary Angles**: Adjacent angles that sum to 180°.

- **Vertical Angles**: Angles that are opposite of each other. They are always congruent (equal in measure).

- **Equilateral Triangle**: All angles are equal.

- **Isosceles Triangle**: Two sides and two angles are equal.

- **Scalene**: No equal angles.

- **Parallel Lines**: Lines that will never intersect. Y **ll** X means line Y is parallel to line X.

- **Perpendicular lines**: Lines that intersect or cross to form 90° angles.

- **Transversal Line**: A line that crosses parallel lines.

- **Bisector**: Any line that cuts a line segment, angle, or polygon exactly in half.

- **Polygon**: Any enclosed plane shape with three or more connecting sides (ex. a triangle).

- **Regular Polygon**: Has all equal sides and equal angles (ex. square).

- **Arc**: A portion of a circle's edge.

- **Chord**: A line segment that connects two different points on a circle.

- **Tangent**: Something that touches a circle at only one point without crossing through it.

- **Sum of Angles**: The sum of angles of a polygon can be calculated using $(n-1)180^\circ$, when n = the number of sides.

Know the Names of Sided Plane Figures:

Number of Sides	Name	Number of Sides	Name
3	Triangle (or Trigon)	11	Hendecagon
4	Quadrilateral (or Tetragon)	12	Dodecagon
5	Pentagon	13	Tridecagon
6	Hexagon	14	Tetradecagon
7	Heptagon	15	Pentadecagon
8	Octagon	16	Hexadecagon
9	Nonagon	17	Heptadecagon

Triangles

The angles in a triangle add up to 180°.
Area of a triangle = ½ * b * h, or ½bh.
Pythagoras' Theorem: $a^2 + b^2 = c^2$.

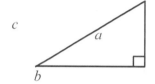

Regular Polygons

Polygon Angle Principle: $S = (n - 2)180$, where S = the sum of interior angles of a polygon with n-sides.

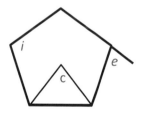

The measure of each central angle (c) is 360°/n.
The measure of each interior angle (i) is $(n - 2)180°/n$.
The measure of each exterior angle (e) is 360°/n.
To compare areas of similar polygons: $A_1/A_2 = (side_1/side_2)^2$

Trapezoids

Four-sided polygon, in which the bases (and only the bases) are parallel.

Isosceles Trapezoid: Base angles are congruent.

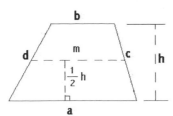

Area and Perimeter of a Trapezoid

$$m = \frac{1}{2}(a + b)$$

$$Area = \frac{1}{2}h * (a + b) = m * h$$

$$Perimeter = a + b + c + d = 2m + c + d$$

If m is the median then: $m \parallel \overline{AB}$ and $m \parallel CD$

Rhombus

Four-sided polygon, in which all four sides are congruent and opposite sides are parallel.

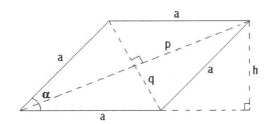

Area and Perimeter of a Rhombus

$$Perimeter = 4a$$

$$Area = a^2 \sin\alpha = a * h = \frac{1}{2}pq$$

$$4a^2 = p^2 + q^2$$

Rectangle

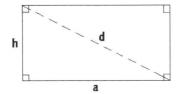

Area and Perimeter of a Rectangle

$$d = \sqrt{a^2 + h^2}$$

$$a = \sqrt{d^2 - h^2}$$

$$h = \sqrt{d^2 - a^2}$$

$$Perimeter = 2a + 2h$$

$$Area = a \cdot h$$

Square

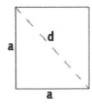

Area and Perimeter of a Square

$$d = a\sqrt{2}$$

$$Perimeter = 4a = 2d\sqrt{2}$$

$$Area = a^2 = \frac{1}{2}d^2$$

Circle

Area and Perimeter of a Circle

$d = 2r$

$Perimeter = 2\pi r = \pi d$

$Area = \pi r^2$

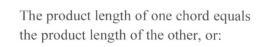

The product length of one chord equals the product length of the other, or:

AB=CD

Area and Perimeter of the Sector of a Circle

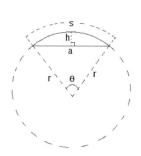

$\alpha = \dfrac{\theta\pi}{180} \; (rad)$

$s = r\alpha$

$Perimeter = 2r + s$

$Area = \dfrac{1}{2}\theta \, r^2 \; (radians) \; or \; \dfrac{n}{360}\pi r^2$

$length \; (l) \; of \; an \; arc \;\; l = \dfrac{\pi n r}{180} \; or \; \dfrac{n}{360}2\pi r$

Area and Perimeter of the Segment of a Circle

$\alpha = \dfrac{\theta\pi}{180} \; (rad)$

$a = 2\sqrt{2hr - h^2}$

$a^2 = 2r^2 - 2r^2 cos\theta$

$s = r\alpha$

$h = r - \dfrac{1}{2}\sqrt{4r^2 - a^2}$

$Perimeter = a + s$

$Area = \dfrac{1}{2}[sr - a(r - h)]$

Cube

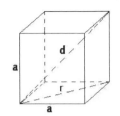

Area and Volume of a Cube

$$r = a\sqrt{2}$$

$$d = a\sqrt{3}$$

$$Area = 6a^2$$

$$Volume = a^3$$

Cuboid

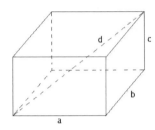

Area and Volume of a Cuboid

$$d = \sqrt{a^2 + b^2 + c^2}$$

$$A = 2(ab + ac + bc)$$

$$V = abc$$

Pyramid

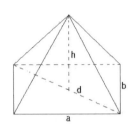

Area and Volume of a Pyramid

$$A_{lateral} = a\sqrt{h^2 + \left(\frac{b}{2}\right)^2} + b\sqrt{h^2 + \left(\frac{a}{2}\right)^2}$$

$$d = \sqrt{a^2 + b^2}$$

$$A_{base} = ab$$

$$A_{total} = A_{lateral} + A_{base}$$

$$V = \frac{1}{3}abh$$

Cylinder

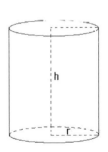

Area and Volume of a Cylinder

$$d = 2r$$

$$A_{surface} = 2\pi rh$$

$$A_{base} = 2\pi r^2$$

$$Area = A_{surface} + A_{base}$$

$$= 2\pi r(h + r)$$

$$Volume = \pi r^2 h$$

Cone

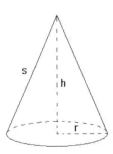

Area and Volume of a Cone

$$d = 2r$$

$$A_{surface} = \pi rs$$

$$A_{base} = \pi r^2$$

$$Area = A_{surface} + A_{base}$$

$$= 2\pi r(h + r)$$

$$Volume = \frac{1}{3}\pi r^2 h$$

Chapter 2: Reading Comprehension

The CASA breaks down the language arts into two sections: Reading and Writing. On the Reading section, you'll have to read passages and answers questions about their content. You might have to identify the main idea of the passage or determine what new information could be added to the passage to bolster the author's argument. The Writing section, on the other hand, focuses on the mechanics of writing. In this section, you'll be asked to identify grammatical errors and revise sentences to make them clearer. You'll also have to write a short essay.

Reading

The Reading section of the CASA will assess your ability to summarize, interpret, and draw conclusions about both non-fiction and fiction passages. You'll be asked questions about:

- the main idea of a passage

- the role of supporting details in the passage

- adding supporting details to the passage

- the structure of the passage

- the author's purpose

- logical inferences that can be drawn from the passage

- comparing passages

- understanding vocabulary and figurative language

The CASA Reading section will require you to read both non-fiction and fiction passages and then answer questions about them. These questions will fall into three main categories:

About the Author
The question will ask about the author's attitude, thoughts, and opinions. When encountering a question asking specifically about the author, pay attention to context clues in the article. The answer may not be explicitly stated but instead conveyed in the overall message.

Passage Facts
You must distinguish between facts and opinions presented in the passage. You may also be asked to identify specific information supplied by the author of the passage.

Additional Information
These questions will have you look at what kind of information could be added to or was missing from the passage. They may also ask in what direction the passage was going. Questions may ask what statement could be added to strengthen the author's statement, or weaken it; they may also provide a fill-in-the-blank option to include a statement that is missing from, but fits with the rest of, the passage.

The Reading section will also include informational source comprehension questions. These questions don't refer back to a text passage; instead, they will ask you to interpret an informational source like a nutrition label, map, or thermometer. (These questions are covered in the section below titled "Informational Source Comprehension.")

Strategies

Despite the different types of questions you will face, there are some strategies for Reading Comprehension which apply across the board:

- Read the answer choices first, then read the passage. This will save you time, as you will know what to look out for as you read.

- Use the process of elimination. Some answer choices are obviously incorrect and are relatively easy to detect. After reading the passage, eliminate those blatantly incorrect answer choices; this increases your chance of finding the correct answer much more quickly.

- Avoid negative statements. Generally, test-makers will not make negative statements about anyone or anything. Statements will be either neutral or positive, so if it seems like an answer choice has a negative connotation, it is very likely that the answer is intentionally false.

The Main Idea

The main idea of a text is the purpose behind why a writer would choose to write a book, article, story, etc. Being able to find and understand the main idea is a critical skill necessary to comprehend and appreciate what you're reading.

Imagine that you're at a friend's home for the evening. He says, "Hey, I think we should watch this movie tonight. Is that ok with you?"

"Yeah, that sounds good," you reply. "What's it about?"

You'd like to know a little about what you'll be watching, but your question may not get you a satisfactory answer, because you've only asked about the topic of the film. The **topic**—what the movie is about—is only half the story. Think, for example, about all the alien invasion films ever been made.

While these films may share the same general subject, what they have to say about the aliens or about humanity's theoretical response to invasion may be very different. Each filmmaker has different ideas or opinions she wants to convey about a topic, just as writers write because they have something to say about a particular topic. When you look beyond the facts to the argument the writer is making about his topic, you're looking for the **main idea**.

One more quick note: the CASA may also ask about a passage's **theme**, which is similar to but distinct from its topic. While a topic is usually a specific *person, place, thing,* or *issue,* the theme is an *idea* or *concept* that the author refers back to frequently. Examples of common themes include ideas like the importance of family, the dangers of technology, and the beauty of nature.

There will be many questions on the CASA that require you to differentiate between the topic, theme, and main idea of a passage. Let's look at an example passage to see how you would answer these questions.

Example:

"Babe Didrikson Zaharias, one of the most decorated female athletes of the twentieth century, is an inspiration for everyone. Born in 1911 in Beaumont, Texas, Zaharias lived in a time when women were considered second-class to men, but she never let that stop her from becoming a champion. Babe was one of seven children in a poor immigrant family, and was competitive from an early age. As a child she excelled at most things she tried, especially sports, which continued into high school and beyond. After high school, Babe played amateur basketball for two years, and soon after began training in track and field. Despite the fact that women were only allowed to enter in three events, Babe represented the United States in the 1932 Los Angeles Olympics, and won two gold medals and one silver for track and field events.

"In the early 1930s, Babe began playing golf which earned her a legacy. The first tournament she entered was a men's only tournament, however she did not make the cut to play. Playing golf as an amateur was the only option for a woman at this time, since there was no professional women's league. Babe played as an amateur for a little over a decade, until she turned pro in 1947 for the Ladies Professional Golf Association (LPGA) of which she was a founding member. During her career as a golfer, Babe won eighty-two tournaments, amateur and professional, including the U.S. Women's Open, All-American Open, and British Women's Open Golf Tournament. In 1953, Babe was diagnosed with cancer, but fourteen weeks later, she played in a tournament. That year she won her third U.S. Women's Open. However by 1955, she didn't have the physicality to compete anymore, and she died of the disease in 1956."

The topic of this paragraph is obviously Babe Zaharias—the whole passage describes events from her life. But what is the main idea of this paragraph? You might be tempted to answer, *Babe Zaharias*, or *Babe Zaharias' life*. Yes, Babe Zaharias' life is the topic of the passage—who or what the passage is about—but the topic is not the main idea. The main idea is what the writer wants to say about this subject. What is the writer saying about Babe Zaharias' life? She's saying that she's someone to admire—that's the main idea and what unites all the information in the paragraph. Lastly, what might the theme of the passage be? The writer refers to several broad concepts, including never giving up and overcoming the odds, both of which could be themes for the passage.

The example above shows two important characteristics of a main idea:

- It is general enough to encompass all of the ideas in the passage. The main idea of a passage should be broad enough for all of the other sentences in that passage to fit underneath it, like people under an umbrella.

- It asserts a specific viewpoint that the author supports with facts, opinions, or other details. In other words, the main idea takes a stand.

Example:

From so far away it's easy to imagine the surface of our solar system's planets as enigmas—how could we ever know what those far-flung planets really look like? It turns out, however, that scientists have a number of tools at their disposal that allow them to paint detailed pictures of many planets' surfaces. The topography of Venus, for example, has been explored by several space probes, including the Russian Venera landers and NASA's Magellan orbiter. These craft used imaging and radar to map the surface of the planet, identifying a whole host of features including volcanoes, craters, and a complex system of channels. Mars has similarly been mapped by space probes, including the famous Mars Rovers, which are automated vehicles that actually landed on the surface of Mars. These rovers have been used by NASA and other space agencies to study the geology, climate, and possible biology of the planet.

In addition these long-range probes, NASA has also used its series of orbiting telescopes to study distant planets. These four massively powerful telescopes include the famous Hubble Space Telescope as well as the Compton Gamma Ray Observatory, Chandra X-Ray Observatory, and the Spitzer Space Telescope. Scientists can use these telescopes to examine planets using not only visible light but also infrared and near-infrared light, ultraviolet light, x-rays and gamma rays.

Powerful telescopes aren't just found in space: NASA makes use of Earth-bound telescopes as well. Scientists at the National Radio Astronomy Observatory in Charlottesville, VA, have spent decades using radio imaging to build an incredibly detailed portrait of Venus' surface. In fact, Earth-bound telescopes offer a distinct advantage over orbiting telescopes because they allow scientists to capture data from a fixed point, which in turn allows them to effectively compare data collected over long period of time.

1. Which of the following sentences best describes the main of the passage?
   a) It's impossible to know what the surfaces of other planets are really like.
   b) Telescopes are an important tool for scientists studying planets in our solar system.
   c) Venus' surface has many of the same features as the Earth's, including volcanoes, craters, and channels.
   d) Scientists use a variety of advanced technologies to study the surface of the planets in our solar system.

Answer:

1. **d)**
   Answer a) can be eliminated because it directly contradicts the rest of the passage, which goes into detail about how scientists have learned about the surfaces of other planets. Answers b) and c) can also be eliminated because they offer only specific details from the passage—while both choices contain details from the passage, neither is general enough to encompass the passage as a whole. Only answer d) provides an assertion that is both backed up by the passage's content and general enough to cover the entire passage.

Topic and Summary Sentences
Writers sometimes lead with preliminary sentences that give the reader clear ideas of what the text is about. A sentence that encompasses the main idea of the text is the topic sentence.
Notice, for example, how the first sentence in the example paragraph about Babe Zaharias states the main idea: *Babe Didrikson Zaharias, one of the most decorated female athletes of the twentieth century, is an inspiration for everyone.*

Topic sentences are often found at the beginning of paragraphs. Sometimes, though, writers begin with specific supporting details and lead up to the main idea; in this case the topic sentence is found at the end of the paragraph. In other cases there isn't a clear topic sentence at all—but that doesn't mean there isn't a main idea; the author has just chosen not to express it in a clear topic sentence. You may also see a

summary sentence at the end of a passage. As its name suggests, this sentence sums up the passage, often by restating the main idea and the author's key evidence supporting it.

Example:

1. In the following paragraph, what are the topic and summary sentences?

   The Constitution of the United States establishes a series of limits to rein in centralized power. Separation of powers distributes federal authority among three competing branches: the executive, the legislative, and the judicial. Checks and balances allow the branches to check the usurpation of power by any one branch. States' rights are protected under the Constitution from too much encroachment by the federal government. Enumeration of powers names the specific and few powers the federal government has. These four restrictions have helped sustain the American republic for over two centuries.

   Answer:

   The topic sentence is the first sentence in the paragraph. It introduces the topic of discussion, in this case the constitutional limits aimed at resisting centralized power. The summary sentence is the last sentence in the paragraph. It sums up the information that was just presented: here, that constitutional limits have helped sustain the United States of America for over two hundred years.

Implied Main Idea

When there's no clear topic sentence, you're looking for an **implied main idea**. This requires some detective work: you will need to look at the author's word choice and tone in addition to the content of the passage to find his or her main idea. Let's look at an example paragraph.

Examples:

One of my summer reading books was *Mockingjay*. Though it's several hundred pages long, I read it in just a few days. I couldn't wait to see what happened to Katniss, the main character. But by the time I got to the end, I wondered if I should have spent my week doing something else. The ending was such a letdown that I completely forgot that I'd enjoyed most of the book.

1. There's no topic sentence here, but you should still be able to find the main idea. Look carefully at what the writer says and how she says it. What is she suggesting?
   a) *Mockingjay* is a terrific novel.
   b) *Mockingjay* is disappointing.
   c) *Mockingjay* is full of suspense.
   d) *Mockingjay* is a lousy novel.

Fortunately, none of Alyssa's coworkers has ever seen inside the large filing drawer in her desk. Disguised by the meticulous neatness of the rest of her workspace, there was no sign of the chaos beneath. To even open it, she had to struggle for several minutes with the enormous pile of junk jamming the drawer, until it would suddenly give way, and papers, folders, and candy wrappers spilled out of the top and onto the floor. It was an organizational nightmare, with torn notes and spreadsheets haphazardly thrown on top of each other, and melted candy smeared across pages.

She was worried the odor would soon permeate to her coworker's desks, revealing to them her secret.

2. Which of the following expresses the main idea of this paragraph?
    a) Alyssa wishes she could move to a new desk.
    b) Alyssa wishes she had her own office.
    c) Alyssa is glad none of her coworkers know about her messy drawer.
    d) Alyssa is sad because she doesn't have any coworkers.

Answers:

1. **b)**
   The correct answer is b): the novel is disappointing. How can you tell that this is the main idea? First, you can eliminate choice c) because it's too specific to be a main idea. It only deals with one specific aspect of the novel (its suspense). Sentences a), b), and d), on the other hand, all express a larger idea about the quality of the novel. However, only one of these statements can actually serve as a "net" for the whole paragraph. Notice that while the first few sentences praise the novel, the last two criticize it. Clearly, this is a mixed review.

   Therefore, the best answer is b). Sentence a) is too positive and doesn't account for the "letdown" of an ending. Sentence d), on the other hand, is too negative and doesn't account for the reader's sense of suspense and interest in the main character. But sentence b) allows for both positive and negative aspects—when a good thing turns bad, we often feel disappointed.

2. **c)**
   What the paragraph adds up to is that Alyssa is terribly embarrassed about her messy drawer, and she's glad that none of her coworkers have seen it, making C) the correct answer choice. This is the main idea. The paragraph opens with the word "fortunately," so we know that she thinks it's a good thing that none of her coworkers have seen inside the drawer. Plus, notice how the drawer is described: "it was an organizational nightmare," and it apparently doesn't even function properly – "to even open the drawer, she had to struggle for several minutes…" The writer reveals that it has an odor, with "melted candy" inside. Alyssa is clearly ashamed of her drawer and worries about what her coworkers would think if they saw inside it.

Supporting Details

Supporting details provide more support for the author's main idea. For instance, in the Babe Zaharias example above, the writer makes the general assertion that *Babe Didrikson Zaharias, one of the most decorated female athletes of the twentieth century, is an inspiration for everyone.* The other sentences offer specific facts and details that prove why Babe Zaharias is an inspiration: the struggles she faced as a female athlete, and the specific years she competed in the Olympics and in golf.

Writers often provide clues that can help you identify supporting details. These **signal words** tell you that a supporting fact or idea will follow, and so can be helpful in identifying supporting details. Signal words can also help you rule out sentences that are not the main idea or topic sentence: if a sentence begins with one of these phrases, it will likely be too specific to be a main idea.

Questions on the CASA will ask you to do two things with supporting details: you will need to find details that support a particular idea and also explain why a particular detail was included in the passage. In order to answer these questions, you need to have a solid understanding of the passage's main idea. With this knowledge, you can determine how a supporting detail fits in with the larger structure of the passage.

Example:

From so far away it's easy to imagine the surface of our solar system's planets as enigmas—how could we ever know what those far-flung planets really look like? It turns out, however, that scientists have a number of tools at their disposal that allow them to paint detailed pictures of many planets' surfaces. The topography of Venus, for example, has been explored by several space probes, including the Russian *Venera* landers and NASA's *Magellan* orbiter. These craft used imaging and radar to map the surface of the planet, identifying a whole host of features including volcanoes, craters, and a complex system of channels. Mars has similarly been mapped by space probes, including the famous Mars Rovers, which are automated vehicles that actually landed on the surface of Mars. These rovers have been used by NASA and other space agencies to study the geology, climate, and possible biology of the planet.

In addition these long-range probes, NASA has also used its series of orbiting telescopes to study distant planets. These four massively powerful telescopes include the famous Hubble Space Telescope as well as the Compton Gamma Ray Observatory, Chandra X-Ray Observatory, and the Spitzer Space Telescope. Scientists can use these telescopes to examine planets using not only visible light but also infrared and near-infrared light, ultraviolet light, x-rays and gamma rays.

Powerful telescopes aren't just found in space: NASA makes use of Earth-bound telescopes as well. Scientists at the National Radio Astronomy Observatory in Charlottesville, VA, have spent decades using radio imaging to build an incredibly detailed portrait of Venus' surface. In fact, Earth-bound telescopes offer a distinct advantage over orbiting telescopes because they allow scientists to capture data from a fixed point, which in turn allows them to effectively compare data collected over long period of time.

1. Which sentence from the text best helps develop the idea that scientists make use of many different technologies to study the surfaces of other planets?
   a) These rovers have been used by NASA and other space agencies to study the geology, climate, and possible biology of the planet.
   b) From so far away it's easy to imagine the surface of our solar system's planets as enigmas—how could we ever know what those far-flung planets really look like?
   c) In addition these long-range probes, NASA has also used its series of orbiting telescopes to study distant planets.
   d) These craft used imaging and radar to map the surface of the planet, identifying a whole host of features including volcanoes, craters, and a complex system of channels.

2. If true, which detail could be added to the passage above to support the author's argument that scientists use many different technologies to study the surface of planets?
   a) Because the Earth's atmosphere blocks x-rays, gamma rays, and infrared radiation, NASA needed to put telescopes in orbit above the atmosphere.
   b) In 2015, NASA released a map of Venus which was created by compiling images from orbiting telescopes and long-range space probes.
   c) NASA is currently using the *Curiosity* and *Opportunity* rovers to look for signs of ancient life on Mars.
   d) NASA has spent over $2.5 billion to build, launch, and repair the Hubble Space Telescope.

3. The author likely included the detail *Earth-bound telescopes offer a distinct advantage over orbiting telescopes because they allow scientists to capture data from a fixed point* in order to:
   a) Explain why it has taken scientists so long to map the surface of Venus.
   b) Suggest that Earth-bound telescopes are the most important equipment used by NASA scientists.
   c) Prove that orbiting telescopes will soon be replaced by Earth-bound telescopes.
   d) Demonstrate why NASA scientists rely on my different types of scientific equipment.

Answers:

1. **c)**
   You're looking for detail from the passage that supports the main idea—scientists make use of many different technologies to study the surfaces of other planets. Answer a) includes a specific detail about rovers, but does not offer any details that support the idea of multiple technologies being used. Similarly, answer d) provides another specific detail about space probes. Answer b) doesn't provide any supporting details; it simply introduces the topic of the passage. Only answer c) provides a detail that directly supports the author's assertion that scientists use multiple technologies to study the planets.

2. **b)**
   You can eliminate answers c) and d) because they don't address the topic of studying the surface of planets. Answer a) can also be eliminated because it only addresses a single technology. Only choice b) provides would add support to the author's claim about the importance of using multiple technologies.

3. **d)**
   Only answer d) directs directly to the author's main argument. The author doesn't mention how long it has taken to map the surface of Venus (answer a), nor does he say that one technology is more important than the others (answer b). And while this detail does highlight the advantages of using Earth-bound telescopes, the author's argument is that many technologies are being used at the same time, so there's no reason to think that orbiting telescopes will be replaced (answer c).

Text Structure

Authors can structure passages in a number of different ways. These distinct organizational patterns, referred to as **text structure**, use the logical relationships between ideas to improve the readability and coherence of a text. The most common ways passages are organized include:

- **problem-solution**: the author presents a problem and then discusses a solution

- **comparison-contrast**: the author presents two situations and then discusses the similarities and differences

- **cause-effect**: the author presents an action and then discusses the resulting effects

- **descriptive**: an idea, object, person, or other item is described in detail

Example:

The issue of public transportation has begun to haunt the fast-growing cities of the southern United States. Unlike their northern counterparts, cities like Atlanta, Dallas, and Houston have long promoted growth out and not up—these are cities full of sprawling suburbs and single-family homes, not densely concentrated skyscrapers and apartments. What to do then, when all those suburbanites need to get into the central business districts for work? For a long time it seemed highways were the answer: twenty-lane wide expanses of concrete that would allow commuters to move from home to work and back again. But these modern miracles have become time-sucking, pollution spewing nightmares. They may not like it, but it's time for these cities to turn toward public transport like trains and buses if they want their cities to remain livable.

1. The organization of this passage can best be described as:
    a) a comparison of two similar ideas
    b) a description of a place
    c) a discussion of several effects all related to the same cause
    d) a discussion of a problem followed by the suggestion of a solution

Answer:

1. **d)**
    You can exclude answer choice c) because the author provides no root cause or a list of effects. From there this question gets tricky, because the passage contains structures similar to those described above. For example, it compares two things (cities in the North and South) and describes a place (a sprawling city). However, if you look at the overall organization of the passage, you can see that it starts by presenting a problem (transportation) and then presents a solution (trains and buses), making answer d) the only choice that encompasses the entire passage.

The Author's Purpose

Whenever an author writes a text, she always has a purpose, whether that's to entertain, inform, explain, or persuade. A short story, for example, is meant to entertain, while an online news article would be designed to inform the public about a current event.

Each of these different types of writing has a specific name. On the CASA, you will be asked to identify which of these categories a passage fits into:

- **Narrative writing** tells a story. (novel, short story, play)

- **Expository writing** informs people. (newspaper and magazine articles)

- **Technical writing** explains something. (product manual, directions)

- **Persuasive writing** tries to convince the reader of something. (opinion column on a blog)

You may also be asked about primary and secondary sources. These terms describe not the writing itself but the author's relationship to what's being written about. A **primary source** is an unaltered piece of writing that was composed during the time when the events being described took place; these texts are often written by the people involved. A **secondary source** might address the same topic but provides extra commentary or analysis. These texts can be written by people not directly involved in the events. For example, a book written by a political candidate to inform people about his or her stand on an issue is a primary source; an online article written by a journalist analyzing how that position will affect the election is a secondary source.

Example:

Elizabeth closed her eyes and braced herself on the armrests that divided her from her fellow passengers. Take-off was always the worst part for her. The revving of the engines, the way her stomach dropped as the plane lurched upward: it made her feel sick. Then, she had to watch the world fade away beneath her, getting smaller and smaller until it was just her and the clouds hurtling through the sky. Sometimes (but only sometimes) it just had to be endured, though. She focused on the thought of her sister's smiling face and her new baby nephew as the plane slowly pulled onto the runway.

1. The passage above is reflective of which type of writing?
   a) Narrative
   b) Expository
   c) Technical
   d) Persuasive

Answer:

1. **a)**
   The passage is telling a story—we meet Elizabeth and learn about her fear of flying—so it's a narrative text (answer a). There is no factual information presented or explained, nor is the author trying to persuade the reader.

Facts vs. Opinions
On the CASA Reading passages you might be asked to identify a statement in a passage as either a fact or an opinion, so you'll need to know the difference between the two. A **fact** is a statement or thought that can be proven to be true. The statement *Wednesday comes after Tuesday* is a fact—you can point to

a calendar to prove it. In contrast, an **opinion** is an assumption that is not based in fact and cannot be proven to be true. The assertion that *television is more entertaining than feature films* is an opinion— people will disagree on this, and there's no reference you can use to prove or disprove it.

Example:
Exercise is critical for healthy development in children. Today, there is an epidemic of unhealthy children in the United States who will face health problems in adulthood due to poor diet and lack of exercise as children. This is a problem for all Americans, especially with the rising cost of healthcare.

It is vital that school systems and parents encourage their children to engage in a minimum of thirty minutes of cardiovascular exercise each day, mildly increasing their heart rate for a sustained period. This is proven to decrease the likelihood of developmental diabetes, obesity, and a multitude of other health problems. Also, children need a proper diet rich in fruits and vegetables so that they can grow and develop physically, as well as learn healthy eating habits early on.

1. Which of the following is a fact in the passage, not an opinion?
   a) Fruits and vegetables are the best way to help children be healthy.
   b) Children today are lazier than they were in previous generations.
   c) The risk of diabetes in children is reduced by physical activity.
   d) Children should engage in thirty minutes of exercise a day.

Answer:

1. **c)**
   Choice b) can be discarded immediately because it is negative and is not discussed anywhere in the passage. Answers a) and d) are both opinions—the author is promoting exercise, fruits, and vegetables as a way to make children healthy. (Notice that these incorrect answers contain words that hint at being an opinion such as *best*, *should*, or other comparisons.) Answer b), on the other hand, is a simple fact stated by the author; it's introduced by the word *proven* to indicate that you don't need to just take the author's word for it.

Drawing Conclusions

In addition to understanding the main idea and factual content of a passage, you'll also be asked to take your analysis one step further and anticipate what other information could logically be added to the passage. In a non-fiction passage, for example, you might be asked which statement the author of the passage would agree with. In an excerpt from a fictional work, you might be asked to anticipate what the character would do next.

To answer these questions, you need to have a solid understanding of the topic, theme, and main idea of the passage; armed with this information, you can figure out which of the answer choices best fits within those criteria (or alternatively, which ones do not). For example, if the author of the passage is advocating for safer working conditions in textile factories, any supporting details that would be added to the passage should support that idea. You might add sentences that contain information about the number of accidents that occur in textile factories or that outline a new plan for fire safety.

Examples:

Today, there is an epidemic of unhealthy children in the United States who will face health problems in adulthood due to poor diet and lack of exercise during their childhood. This is a problem for all Americans, as adults with chronic health issues are adding to the rising cost of healthcare. A child who grows up living an unhealthy lifestyle is likely to become an adult who does the same.

Because exercise is critical for healthy development in children, it is vital that school systems and parents encourage their children to engage in a minimum of thirty minutes of cardiovascular exercise each day. Even this small amount of exercise has been proven to decrease the likelihood that young people will develop diabetes, obesity, and other health issues as adults. In addition to exercise, children need a proper diet rich in fruits and vegetables so that they can grow and develop physically. Starting a good diet early also teaches children healthy eating habits they will carry into adulthood.

1. The author of this passage would most likely agree with which statement?
   a) Parents are solely responsible for the health of their children.
   b) Children who do not want to exercise should not be made to.
   c) Improved childhood nutrition will help lower the amount Americans spend on healthcare.
   d) It's not important to teach children healthy eating habits because they will learn them as adults.

Elizabeth closed her eyes and braced herself on the armrests that divided her from her fellow passengers. Take-off was always the worst part for her. The revving of the engines, the way her stomach dropped as the plane lurched upward: it made her feel sick. Then, she had to watch the world fade away beneath her, getting smaller and smaller until it was just her and the clouds hurtling through the sky. Sometimes (but only sometimes) it just had to be endured, though. She focused on the thought of her sister's smiling face and her new baby nephew as the plane slowly pulled onto the runway.

2. Which of the following is Elizabeth least likely to do in the future?
   a) Take a flight to her brother's wedding.
   b) Apply for a job as a flight attendant.
   c) Never board an airplane again.
   d) Get sick on an airplane.

Answers:

1. **c)**
   The author would most likely support answer c): he mentions in the first paragraph that unhealthy habits are adding to the rising cost of healthcare. The main idea of the passage is that nutrition and exercise are important for children, so answer b) doesn't make sense—the author would likely support measures to encourage children to exercise. Answers a) and d) can also be eliminated because they are directly contradicted in the text. The author specifically mentions the role of schools systems, so he doesn't believe parents are solely responsible for their children's health. He also specifically states that

children who grow up with unhealthy habit will become adults with unhealthy habits, which contradicts d).

2. **b)**
It's clear from the passage that Elizabeth hates flying, but it willing to endure it for the sake of visiting her family. Thus, it seems likely that she would be willing to get on a plane for her brother's wedding, making a) and c) incorrect answers. The passage also explicitly tells us that she feels sick on planes, so d) is likely to happen. We can infer, though, that she would not enjoy being on an airplane for work, so she's very unlikely to apply for a job as a flight attendant, which is choice b).

Meaning of Words and Phrases

On the Reading section you may also be asked to provide definitions or intended meanings for words within passages. You may have never encountered some of these words before the test, but there are tricks you can use to figure out what they mean.

Context Clues
The most fundamental vocabulary skill is using the context in which a word is used to determine its meaning. Your ability to observe sentences closely is extremely useful when it comes to understanding new vocabulary words.

There are two types of context that can help you understand the meaning of unfamiliar words: situational context and sentence context. Regardless of which context is present, these types of questions are not really testing your knowledge of vocabulary; rather, they test your ability to comprehend the meaning of a word through its usage.

Situational context is context that is presented by the setting or circumstances in which a word or phrase occurs. **Sentence context** occurs within the specific sentence that contains the vocabulary word. To figure out words using sentence context clues, you should first determine the most important words in the sentence.

There are four types of clues that can help you understand context, and therefore the meaning of a word:

- **Restatement** clues occur when the definition of the word is clearly stated in the sentence.

- **Positive/negative clues** can tell you whether a word has a positive or negative meaning.

- **Contrast clues** include the opposite meaning of a word. Words like *but, on the other hand,* and *however* are tip-offs that a sentence contains a contrast clue.

- **Specific detail clues** provide a precise detail that can help you understand the meaning of the word.

It is important to remember that more than one of these clues can be present in the same sentence. The more there are, the easier it will be to determine the meaning of the word. For example, the following sentence uses both restatement and positive/negative clues: *Janet suddenly found herself destitute, so poor she could barely afford to eat.* The second part of the sentence clearly indicates that *destitute* is a negative word. It also restates the meaning: very poor.

Examples:

1. I had a hard time reading her *illegible* handwriting.
    a) neat
    b) unsafe
    c) sloppy
    d) educated

2. The dog was *dauntless* in the face of danger, braving the fire to save the girl trapped inside the building.
    a) difficult
    b) fearless
    c) imaginative
    d) startled

3. Beth did not spend any time preparing for the test, but Tyrone kept a *rigorous* study schedule.
    a) strict
    b) loose
    c) boring
    d) strange

Answers:

1. **c)**
   Already, you know that this sentence is discussing something that is hard to read. Look at the word that *illegible* is describing: handwriting. Based on context clues, you can tell that *illegible* means that her handwriting is hard to read.
   Next, look at the answer choices. Choice a), *neat,* is obviously a wrong answer because neat handwriting would not be difficult to read. Choices b) and d), *unsafe* and *educated,* don't make sense. Therefore, choice c), *sloppy,* is the best answer.

2. **b)**
   Demonstrating bravery in the face of danger would be b) *fearless*. In this case, the restatement clue (*braving the fire*) tells you exactly what the word means.

3. **a)**
   In this case, the contrast word *but* tells us that Tyrone studied in a different way than Beth, which means it's a contrast clue. If Beth did not study hard, then Tyrone did. The best answer, therefore, is choice a).

Analyzing Words

As you no doubt know, determining the meaning of a word can be more complicated than just looking in a dictionary. A word might have more than one **denotation**, or definition; which one the author intends can only be judged by looking at the surrounding text. For example, the word *quack* can refer to the sound a duck makes, or to a person who publicly pretends to have a qualification which he or she does not actually possess.

A word may also have different **connotations**, which are the implied meanings and emotion a word evokes in the reader. For example, a cubicle is a simply a walled desk in an office, but for many the word implies a constrictive, uninspiring workplace. Connotations can vary greatly between cultures and even between individuals.

Lastly, authors might make use of **figurative language**, which is the use of a word to imply something other than the word's literal definition. This is often done by comparing two things. If you say *I felt like a butterfly when I got a new haircut*, the listener knows you don't resemble an insect but instead felt beautiful and transformed.

Word Structure

Although you are not expected to know every word in the English language for your test, you will need the ability to use deductive reasoning to find the choice that is the best match for the word in question, which is why we are going to explain how to break a word into its parts to determine its meaning. Many words can be broken down into three main parts:

prefix – root – suffix

Roots are the building blocks of all words. Every word is either a root itself or has a root. Just as a plant cannot grow without roots, neither can vocabulary, because a word must have a root to give it meaning. The root is what is left when you strip away all the prefixes and suffixes from a word. For example, in the word *unclear*, if you take away the prefix *un-*, you have the root *clear*.

Roots are not always recognizable words, because they generally come from Latin or Greek words, such as *nat*, a Latin root meaning born. The word *native*, which means a person born in a referenced placed, comes from this root, so does the word *prenatal*, meaning before birth. It's important to keep in mind, however, that roots do not always match the exact definitions of words, and they can have several different spellings.

Prefixes are syllables added to the beginning of a word and **suffixes** are syllables added to the end of the word. Both carry assigned meanings and can be attached to a word to completely change the word's meaning or to enhance the word's original meaning.

Let's use the word prefix itself as an example: *fix* means to place something securely and *pre-* means before. Therefore, *prefix* means to place something before or in front. Now let's look at a suffix: in the word *feminism*, *femin* is a root which means female. The suffix *-ism* means act, practice, or process. Thus, *feminism* is the process of establishing equal rights for women.

Although you cannot determine the meaning of a word by a prefix or suffix alone, you can use this knowledge to eliminate answer choices; understanding whether the word is positive or negative can give you the partial meaning of the word.

Comparing Passages

In addition to analyzing single passages, the CASA will also require you to compare two passages. Usually these passage will discuss the same topic, and it will be your task to identify the similarities and differences between the authors' main ideas, supporting details, and tone.

Examples:

Read the two passage below and answer the following questions.

Passage 1

Today, there is an epidemic of unhealthy children in the United States who will face health problems in adulthood due to poor diet and lack of exercise during their childhood: in 2012, the Centers for Disease Control found that 18 percent of students aged 6 – 11 were obese. This is a problem for all Americans, as adults with chronic health issues are adding to the rising cost of healthcare. A child who grows up living an unhealthy lifestyle is likely to become an adult who does the same.

Because exercise is critical for healthy development in children, it is vital that school systems and parents encourage their children to engage in a minimum of thirty minutes of cardiovascular exercise each day. Even this small amount of exercise has been proven to decrease the likelihood that young people will develop diabetes, obesity, and other health issues as adults. In addition to exercise, children need a proper diet rich in fruits and vegetables so that they can grow and develop physically. Starting a good diet early also teaches children healthy eating habits they will carry into adulthood.

Passage 2

When was the last time you took a good, hard look at a school lunch? For many adults, it's probably been years—decades even—since they last thought about students' midday meals. If they did stop to ponder, they might picture something reasonably wholesome if not very exciting: a peanut butter and jelly sandwich paired with an apple, or a traditional meat-potatoes-and-veggies plate. At worst, they may think, kids are making due with some pizza and a carton of milk.

The truth, though, is that many students aren't even getting the meager nutrients offered up by a simple slice of pizza. Instead, schools are serving up heaping helpings of previously frozen, recently fried delicacies like french fries and chicken nuggets. These high-carb, low-protein options are usually paired with a limp, flavorless, straight-from-the-freezer vegetable that quickly gets tossed in the trash. And that carton of milk? It's probably a sugar-filled chocolate sludge, or it's been replaced with a student's favorite high-calorie soda.

So what, you might ask. Kids like to eat junk food—it's a habit they'll grow out of soon enough. Besides, parents can always pack lunches for students looking for something better. But is that really the lesson we want to be teaching our kids? Many of those children aren't going to grow out of bad habits; they're going to reach adulthood thinking that ketchup is a vegetable. And students in low-income families are particularly impacted by the sad state of school food. These parents rely on schools to provide a warm, nutritious meal because they don't have the time or money to prepare food at home. Do we really want to be punishing these children with soggy meat patties and salt-soaked potato chips?

1. Both authors are arguing for the important of improving childhood nutrition. How do the authors' strategies differ?
    a) Passage 1 presents several competing viewpoints while Passage 2 offers a single argument.
    b) Passage 1 uses scientific data while Passage 2 uses figurative language.
    c) Passage 1 is descriptive while Passage 2 uses a cause and effect structure.
    d) Passage 1 has a friendly tone while the tone of Passage 2 is angry.

2. Both authors argue that
    a) Children should learn healthy eating habits at a young age.
    b) Low-income students are disproportionately affected by the low-quality food offered in schools.
    c) Teaching children about good nutritious will lower their chances of developing diabetes as adults.
    d) Schools should provide children an opportunity to exercise every day.

Answers:

1. **b)**
    The first author uses scientific facts (*the Centers for Disease Control found . . .* and *Even this small amount of exercise has been proven . . .*) to back up his argument, while the second uses figurative language (the ironic *delicacies* and the metaphor *sugar-filled chocolate sludge*), so the correct answer is b). Answer a) is incorrect because the first author does present any opposing viewpoints. Answer c) is incorrect because Passage 2 does not have a cause and effect structure. And while the author of the first passage could be described as angry, the first author is not particularly friendly, so you can eliminate answer d) as well.

2. **a)**
    Both authors argue children should learn healthy eating habits at a young age (answer a). The author of Passage 1 states that *a child who grows up living an unhealthy lifestyle is likely to become an adult who does the same*, and the author of Passage 2 states that *many of those children aren't going to grow out of bad habits*—both of these sentences argue that it's necessary to teach children about nutrition early in life. Answers c) and d) are mentioned only by the author of Passage 1, and answer b) is only discussed in Passage 2.

Chapter 3: Writing

MULTIPLE-CHOICE

The multiple-choice questions in the Writing section will cover: Error Identification, in which you'll need to recognize errors in sentence structure, grammar, and syntax; Sentence Improvement, wherein, as the name suggests, you will be given choices to improve a presented sentence; and Paragraph Improvement, which will test your ability to revise sentences in a larger context.

Many of the concepts which you reviewed in the previous chapter are applicable to this chapter as well. We'll provide a brief review of those concepts with which you'll need to be familiar that were not covered in Chapter 2.

Nouns, Pronouns, Verbs, Adjectives, and Adverbs

Nouns
Nouns are people, places, or things. They are typically the subject of a sentence. For example, "The hospital was very clean." The noun is "hospital;" it is the "place."

Pronouns
Pronouns essentially "replace" nouns. This allows a sentence to not sound repetitive. Take the sentence: "Sam stayed home from school because Sam was not feeling well." The word "Sam" appears twice in the same sentence. Instead, you can use a pronoun and say, "Sam stayed at home because *he* did not feel well." Sounds much better, right?

Most Common Pronouns:

- I, me, mine, my.

- You, your, yours.

- He, him, his.

- She, her, hers.

- It, its.

- We, us, our, ours.

- They, them, their, theirs.

Verbs
Remember the old commercial, "Verb: It's what you do"? That sums up verbs in a nutshell! Verbs are the "action" of a sentence; verbs "do" things.

They can, however, be quite tricky. Depending on the subject of a sentence, the tense of the word (past, present, future, etc.), and whether or not they are regular or irregular, verbs have many variations.

Example: "He runs to second base." The verb is "runs." This is a "regular verb."

Example: "I am 7 years old." The verb in this case is "am." This is an "irregular verb."

As mentioned, verbs must use the correct tense – and that tense must remain the same throughout the sentence. "I was baking cookies and eat some dough." That sounded strange, didn't it? That's because the two verbs "baking" and "eat" are presented in different tenses. "Was baking" occurred in the past; "eat," on the other hand, occurs in the present. Instead, it should be "**ate** some dough."

Adjectives

Adjectives are words that describe a noun and give more information. Take the sentence: "The boy hit the ball." If you want to know more about the noun "boy," then you could use an adjective to describe it. "The **little** boy hit the ball." An adjective simply provides more information about a noun or subject in a sentence.

Adverb

For some reason, many people have a difficult time with adverbs – but don't worry! They are really quite simple. Adverbs are similar to adjectives in that they provide more information about a part of a sentence; however, they do **not** describe nouns – that's an adjective's job. Instead, adverbs describe verbs, adjectives, and even other adverbs.

Take the sentence: "The doctor said she hired a new employee."

It would give more information to say: "The doctor said she **recently** hired a new employee." Now we know more about *how* the action was executed. Adverbs typically describe when or how something has happened, how it looks, how it feels, etc.

Good vs. Well

A very common mistake that people make concerning adverbs is the misuse of the word "good."

"Good" is an adjective – things taste good, look good, and smell good. "Good" can even be a noun – "Superman does good" – when the word is speaking about "good" vs. "evil." HOWEVER, "good" is never an adverb.

People commonly say things like, "I did really good on that test," or, "I'm good." Ugh! This is NOT the correct way to speak! In those sentences, the word "good" is being used to describe an action: how a person **did**, or how a person **is**. Therefore, the adverb "well" should be used. "I did really **well** on that test." "I'm **well**."

The correct use of "well" and "good" can make or break a person's impression of your grammar – make sure to always speak correctly!

Study Tips for Improving Vocabulary and Grammar

1. You're probably pretty computer savvy and know the Internet very well. Visit the Online Writing Lab website, which is sponsored by Purdue University, at http://owl.english.purdue.edu. This site provides you with an excellent overview of syntax, writing style, and strategy. It also has helpful and lengthy review sections that include multiple-choice "Test Your Knowledge" quizzes, which provide immediate answers to the questions.

2. It's beneficial to read the entire passage first to determine its intended meaning BEFORE you attempt to answer any questions. Doing so provides you with key insight into a passage's syntax (especially verb tense, subject-verb agreement, modifier placement, writing style, and punctuation).

3. When you answer a question, use the "Process-of-Elimination Method" to determine the best answer. Try each of the four answers and determine which one BEST fits with the meaning of the paragraph. Find the BEST answer. Chances are that the BEST answer is the CORRECT answer.

Practice Sentence Improvement

To give you a better idea of what you can expect from this section of the CASA, here are a few sample sentence improvement questions.

Paragraph A
(1) Of the two types of eclipses, the most common is the lunar eclipse, which occurs when a full moon passes through Earth's shadow. (2) The disc-shaped moon slowly disappears completely or turns a coppery red color. (3) Solar and lunar eclipses both occur from time to time.

Paragraph B
(4) During a solar eclipse, the moon passes between the Earth and Sun. (5) As the moon moves into alignment, it blocks the light from the Sun creating an eerie darkness. (6) When the moon is perfectly in position, the Sun's light is visible as a ring, or corona, around the dark disc of the moon. (7) A lunar eclipse can be viewed from anywhere on the nighttime half of Earth, a solar eclipse can only be viewed from a zone that is only about 200 miles wide and covers about one-half of a percent of Earth's total area.

1. Sentence 1: "Of the two types of eclipses, the most common is the lunar eclipse, which occurs when a full moon passes through Earth's shadow." What correction should be made to this sentence?
   a) Change "most" to "more."
   b) Change "occurs" to "occur."
   c) Change "which" to "that."
   d) Change "Earth's" to "Earths'."
   e) No correction is necessary.

2. Sentence 2: "The disc-shaped moon slowly disappears completely or turns a coppery red color." If you rewrote sentence 2, beginning with "The disc-shaped moon slowly turns a coppery red color," the next word should be:

 a) And.
 b) But.
 c) When.
 d) Because.
 e) Or.

3. Which revision would improve the effectiveness of paragraph A?

 a) Remove sentence 1.
 b) Move sentence 2 to the beginning of the paragraph.
 c) Remove sentence 2.
 d) Move sentence 3 to the beginning of the paragraph.
 e) No revision is necessary.

4. Sentence 7: "A lunar eclipse can be viewed from anywhere on the nighttime half of Earth, a solar eclipse can only be viewed from a zone that is only about 200 miles wide and covers about one-half of a percent of Earth's total area." Which of the following is the best way to write the underlined portion of this sentence? If the original is the best way, choose option **a)**.

 a) "Earth, a solar eclipse"
 b) "Earth a solar eclipse"
 c) "Earth; a solar eclipse"
 d) "Earth, because a solar eclipse"
 e) "Earth, when a solar eclipse"

Answers:

1. a)

Use the comparative "more" when comparing only two things. Here, you comparing two types of eclipses, so "more" is correct. The other changes introduce errors.

2. e)

The clauses are joined by the conjunction "or" in the original sentence. Maintaining this conjunction maintains the original relationship between ideas.

3. d)

As sentence 3 would serve as a good topic sentence, as well as an effective lead into sentence 1, the paragraph could be improved by moving sentence 3 to the beginning.

4. c)

The two related sentences should be separated by a semicolon. The other answers introduce incorrect punctuation or an inaccurate relationship between the sentences.

THE WRITING SAMPLE

During this portion of the test, you will be provided a prompt, for which you will need to write a short response essay. You will need to write an essay that is focused, organized, well-developed and supported, free of errors (usage, spelling, mechanics), and that has proper sentence structure.

This may sound like a tall order, but you can do it! The only way to prepare for this section is to practice writing timed essays. Your essay will be read by two different people, and given two separate scores from 1 to 6 (6 being the highest). If the response is so unrelated to the topic, is illegible, or even written in a language other than English, the section will not receive a grade.

An Effective Essay Demonstrates:

1. Insightful and effective development of a point-of-view on the issue.

2. Critical thinking skills. For example: Two oppositions are given; instead of siding with one, you provide examples in which both would be appropriate.

3. Organization. It is clearly focused and displays a smooth progression of ideas.

4. Supportive information. If a statement is made, it is followed by examples, reasons, or other supporting evidence.

5. Skillful use of varied, accurate, and apt vocabulary.

6. Sentence variety. (Not every sentence follows a "subject-verb" pattern. Mix it up!)

7. Proper grammar and spelling.

Essay Examples and Evaluations

Here we will provide a sample essay prompt, followed by four short sample responses. The four sample responses each display different qualities of work; an explanation will follow each sample, explaining what score it would have earned and why.

Prompt:
Research tells us that what children learn in their earliest years is very important to their future success in school. Because of this, public schools all over the country are starting to offer Pre-Kindergarten classes.

What are the benefits of starting school early? What are some of the problems you see in sending four-year-olds to school?

Write a composition in which you weigh the pros and cons of public school education for Pre-Kindergartners. Give reasons and specific examples to support your opinion. There is no specific word limit for your composition, but it should be long enough to give a clear and complete presentation of your ideas.

Sample Score 5-6 Essay

Today, more and more four-year-olds are joining their big brothers and sisters on the school bus and going to Pre-Kindergarten. Although the benefits of starting school early are clear, it is also clear that Pre-K is not for every child.

The students who are successful in Pre-K are ahead when they start kindergarten. Pre-K teaches them to play well with others. Even though it does not teach skills like reading and writing, it does help to prepare students for "real" school. Pre-K students sing songs, dance, paint and draw, climb and run. They learn to share and to follow directions. They tell stories and answer questions, and as they do, they add new words to their vocabularies. Pre-K can also give students experiences they might not get at home. They might take trips to the zoo or the farm, have visits from musicians or scientists, and so on. These experiences help the students better understand the world.

There are, however, some real differences among children of this age. Some four-year-olds are just not ready for the structure of school life. Some have a hard time leaving home, even for only three or four hours a day. Other children may already be getting a great preschool education at home or in daycare.

While you weigh the advantages and disadvantages of Pre-K, it is safe to say that each child is different. For some children, it is a wonderful introduction to the world of school. But others may not or should not be forced to attend Pre-K.

Evaluation of Sample Score 5-6 Essay
This paper is clearly organized and has stated a definite point of view. The paper opens with an introduction and closes with a conclusion. The introduction and conclusion combine an expression of the writer's opinion. Connections to the writer's opinion are made throughout the paper.

Sample Score 3-4 Essay

Just like everything in life, there are pros and cons to early childhood education. Pre-K classes work for many children, but they aren't for everyone. The plusses of Pre-K are obvious. Pre-K children learn many skills that will help them in kindergarten and later on. Probably the most important thing they learn is how to follow directions. This is a skill they will need at all stages of their life.

Other plusses include simple tasks like cutting, coloring in the lines, and learning capital letters. Many children don't get these skills at home. They need Pre-K to prepare them for kindergarten.

The minuses of Pre-K are not as obvious, but they are real. Children at this young age need the comfort of home. They need to spend time with parents, not strangers. They need that security. If parents are able to, they can give children the background they need to do well in school.

Other minuses include the fact that a lot of four year-old children can't handle school. They don't have the maturaty to sit still, pay attention, or share with others. Given another year, they may mature enough to do just fine in school. Sometimes it's better just to wait.

So there are definitely good things about Pre-K programs in our public schools, and I would definitely want to see one in our local schools. However, I think parents should decide whether their children are ready for a Pre-K education or not.

Evaluation of Sample Score 3-4 Essay

This paper has an identifiable organization plan, with pros and cons listed in order. The development is easy to understand, if not somewhat simplistic. The language of the paper is uneven, with some vague turns of phrase: "Just like everything in life," "definitely some good things." The word "maturity" is also misspelled. However, the essay is clear and controlled, and generally follows written conventions. If the writer had included more developed and explicit examples and used more varied words, this paper might have earned a higher score.

Sample Score 1-2 Essay

Is early childhood education a good idea? It depends on the child you're talking about. Some children probally need more education in the early years and need something to do to keep out of trouble. Like if there isnt any good nursry school or day care around it could be very good to have Pre-Kindergarten at the school so those children could have a good start on life. A lot of skills could be learned in Pre-Kindergarten, for example they could learn to write their name, cut paper, do art, etc.

Of course theres some kids who wouldnt do well, acting out and so on, so they might do better staying home than going to Pre-Kindergarten, because they just arent ready for school, and maybe wouldn't even be ready for kindergarten the next year either. Some kids just act younger than others or are too baby-ish for school.

So I would suport Pre-Kindergarten in our schools, it seems like a good idea to have someplace for those kids to go. Even if some kids wouldnt do well I think enough kids would do well, and it would make a diference in their grades as they got older. All those skills that they learned would help them in the future. If we did have Pre-Kindergarten it would help their working parents too, knowing their kids were someplace safe and learning importent things for life.

Evaluation of Sample Score 1-2 Essay
Although the writer of this paper has some good points to make, a lack of language skills, considerable misspellings, and a certain disconnectedness of thought keep the paper from scoring high. The paper begins with a vague introduction of the topic and ends with a paragraph that expresses the author's opinion, but the rest of the paper is disorganized. The reasons given do not always have examples to support them, and the examples that are given are weak.

Sample Score 1 Essay

What are benefits? What are some of problems with sending four-year-olds to school? Well, for one problem, its hard to see how little kids would do with all those big kids around at the school. They might get bullyed or lern bad habits, so I wouldnt want my four year old around those big kids on the bus and so on. Its hard to see how that could be good for a four year old. In our area we do have Pre-Kindergarten at our school but you dont have to go there a lot of kids in the program, I think about 50 or more, you see them a lot on the play ground mostly all you see them do is play around so its hard to see how that could be too usefull. They could play around at home just as easy. A reason for not doing Pre-Kindergarten is then what do you learn in Kindergarten. Why go do the same thing two years when you could just do one year when your a little bit bigger (older). I wonder do the people who want Pre-Kindergarten just want there kids out of the house or a baby sitter for there kids. Its hard to see why do we have to pay for that. I dont even know if Kindergarten is so usefull anyway, not like first grade where you actually learn something. So I would say theres lots of problems with Pre-Kindergarten.

Evaluation of Sample Score 1 Essay

This paper barely responds to the prompt. It gives reasons not to support Pre-K instruction, but it does not present any benefits of starting school early. The writer repeats certain phrases ("It's hard to see") to no real effect, and the faulty spelling, grammar, and punctuation significantly impede understanding. Several sentences wander off the topic entirely ("there a lot of kids in the program, I think about 50 or more, you see them a lot on the playground.", "I dont even know if Kindergarten is so usefull anyway, not like first grade where you actually learn something."). Instead of opening with an introduction, the writer simply lifts phrases from the prompt. The conclusion states the writer's opinion, but the reasons behind it are illogical and vague. Rather than organizing the essay in paragraph form, the writer has written a single, run-on paragraph. The lack of organization, weak language skills, and failure to address the prompt earn this essay a 2.

Practice Test 1

Mathematics

Section 1:
Percent/Part/Whole; Percent Change

Section 2:
Mean, Median, Mode

Section 3:
Exponents and Roots

Section 4:
Algebraic Equations

Section 5:
Inequalities, Literal Equations, Polynomials, Binomials

Section 6:
Slope and Distance to Midpoint

Section 7:
Absolute Value Equations

Section 8:
Geometry

Section 9:
Fundamental Counting Principle, Permutations, Combinations

Section 10:
Ratios, Proportions, Rate of Change

Percent/Part/Whole, Percent Change

1. In a class of 42 students, 18 are boys. Two girls get transferred to another school. What percent of students remaining are girls?
   a. 14%.
   b. 16%.
   c. 52.4%.
   d. 60%.
   e. None of the above.

2. A payroll check is issued for $500.00. If 20% goes to bills, 30% of the remainder goes to pay entertainment expenses, and 10% of what is left is placed in a retirement account, then approximately how much is remaining?
   a. $150.
   b. $250.
   c. $170.
   d. $350.
   e. $180.

3. A painting by Van Gogh increased in value by 80% from year 1995 to year 2000. If in year 2000, the painting is worth $7200, what was its value in 1995?
   a. $1500.
   b. $2500.
   c. $3000.
   d. $4000.
   e. $5000.

4. "Dresses and Ties" sells a particular dress for $60 dollars. But, they decide to discount the price of that dress by 25%. How much does the dress cost now?
   a. $55.
   b. $43.
   c. $45.
   d. $48.
   e. $65.

5. A sweater goes on sale for 30% off. If the original price was $70, what is the discounted price?
   a. $48.
   b. $49.
   c. $51.
   d. $65.
   e. $52.

Mean, Median, Mode

1. If test A is taken 5 times with an average result of 21, and test B is taken 13 times with an average result of 23, what is the combined average?
   a. 22.24.
   b. 22.22.
   c. 22.00.
   d. 22.44.
   e. 24.22.

2. A set of data has 12 entries. The average of the first 6 entries is 12, the average of the next two entries is 20, and the average of the remaining entries is 4. What is the average of the entire data set?
   a. 10.
   b. 10.67.
   c. 11.
   d. 12.67.
   e. 10.5.

3. What is the average score of 8 tests where the score for 3 tests is 55, the score for two tests is 35, and the remaining tests have scores of 70?
   a. 50.3.
   b. 52.5.
   c. 55.1.
   d. 56.0.
   e. 55.6.

4. The temperatures over a week are recorded as follows:

Day	High	Low
Monday	80	45
Tuesday	95	34
Wednesday	78	47
Thursday	79	55
Friday	94	35
Saturday	67	46
Sunday	76	54

What is the approximate average high temperature and average low temperature during the week?
   a. 90, 50.
   b. 80, 40.
   c. 81, 45.
   d. 82, 46.
   e. 81, 47.

Exponents and Roots

1. What is $x^2y^3z^5/y^2z^{-9}$?
   a. y^5z^4.
   b. yz^4.
   c. x^2yz^{14}.
   d. $x^2y^5z^4$.
   e. xyz.

2. What is k if $(2m^3)^5 = 32m^{k+1}$?
   a. 11.
   b. 12.
   c. 13.
   d. 14.
   e. 15.

3. What is $x^5y^4z^3/x^{-3}y^2z^{-4}$?
   a. $x^6y^4z^7$.
   b. x^8yz^7.
   c. x^6yz^7.
   d. $x^8y^2z^7$.
   e. $x^6y^2z^7$.

Algebraic Equations

1. The number $568cd$ should be divisible by 2, 5, and 7. What are the values of the digits c and d?
   a. 56835.
   b. 56830.
   c. 56860.
   d. 56840.
   e. 56800.

2. Carla is 3 times older than her sister Megan. Eight years ago, Carla was 18 years older than her sister. What is Megan's age?
   a. 10.
   b. 8.
   c. 9.
   d. 6.
   e. 5.

3. What is the value of $f(x) = (x^2 - 25)/(x + 5)$ when $x = 0$?
   a. -1.
   b. -2.
   c. -3.
   d. -4.
   e. -5.

4. Four years from now, John will be twice as old as Sally will be. If Sally was 10 eight years ago, how old is John?
    a. 35.
    b. 40.
    c. 45.
    d. 50.
    e. 55.

5. I have some marbles. I give 25% to Vic, 20% to Robbie, 10% to Jules. I then give 6/20 of the remaining amount to my brother, and keep the rest for myself. If I end up with 315 marbles, how many did I have to begin with?
    a. 1000.
    b. 1500.
    c. 3500.
    d. 400.
    e. 500.

6. I have some marbles. I give 25% to Vic, 20% of the remainder to Robbie, 10% of that remainder to Jules and myself I then give 6/20 of the remaining amount to my brother, and keep the rest for myself. If I end up with 315 marbles, how many did I have to begin with?
    a. 800.
    b. 833.
    c. 834.
    d. 378.
    e. 500.

7. If $x = 5y + 4$, what is the value of y if $x = 29$?
    a. 33/5.
    b. 5.5.
    c. 5.
    d. 0.
    e. 29/5.

8. A bag of marbles has 8 marbles. If I buy 2 bags of marbles, how many more bags of marbles would I need to buy to have a total of at least 45 marbles?
    a. 3.
    b. 4.
    c. 5.
    d. 6.
    e. 29.

9. A factory that produces widgets wants to sell them each for $550. It costs $50 for the raw materials for each widget, and the startup cost for the factory was $10000. How many widgets have to be sold so that the factory can break even?
    a. 10.
    b. 20.
    c. 30.
    d. 40.
    e. 50.

Inequalities, Literal Equations, Polynomials, and Binomials

1. If $x < 5$ and $y < 6$, then $x + y \ \underline{\ ?\ } \ 11$.
    a. $<$
    b. $>$
    c. $\leq$
    d. $\geq$
    e. $=$

2. Which of the following is true about the inequality $25x^2 - 40x - 32 < 22$?
    a. There are no solutions.
    b. There is a set of solutions.
    c. There is 1 solution only.
    d. There are 2 solutions.
    e. There are 3 solutions.

3. If $x - 2y > 6$, what possible values of y always have x as greater than or equal to 2?
    a. $y \geq 1$.
    b. $y \leq 0$.
    c. $y \geq -2$.
    d. $y < 2$.
    e. $y \leq 6$.

4. Find the point of intersection of the lines $x + 2y = 4$ and $3x - y = 26$.
    a. $(1, 3)$.
    b. $(8, -2)$.
    c. $(0, 2)$.
    d. $(2, -1)$.
    e. $(4, 26)$.

5. If $a + b = 2$, and $a - b = 4$, what is a?
    a. 1.
    b. 2.
    c. 3.
    d. 4.
    e. 5.

6. If $\sqrt{a} + \sqrt{b} = 2$, and $\sqrt{a} - \sqrt{b} = 3$, what is $a + b$?
    a. 6.5.
    b. 6.
    c. 5.5.
    d. 5.
    e. 4.5.

Slope and Distance to Midpoint

1. What is the equation of the line that passes through (3, 5), with intercept $y = 8$?
    a. $y = x + 8$.
    b. $y = x - 8$.
    c. $y = -x - 8$.
    d. $y = -x + 8$.
    e. $y = -x$.

2. What is the value of y in the equation $(3x - 4)^2 = 4y - 15$, if $x = 3$?
    a. 10.
    b. 2.5.
    c. -10.
    d. -2.5.
    e. 5.

3. If $y = 4x + 6y$, what is the range of y if $-10 < x \leq 5$?
    a. $-4 < y \leq 8$.
    b. $-4 < y < 8$.
    c. $8 > y > -4$.
    d. $-4 \leq y < 8$.
    e. $-4 \leq y \leq 8$.

4. If Jennifer gets three times as much allowance as Judy gets, and Judy gets \$5/week, how much does Jennifer get every month?
    a. \$15.
    b. \$20.
    c. \$30.
    d. \$45.
    e. \$60.

5. What is the value of x, if $y = 8$ in the equation $5x + 9y = 3x - 6y + 5$?
    a. 57.5.
    b. 60.
    c. -60.
    d. -57.5.
    e. None of the above.

6.

A (3, 5) 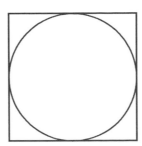 B (8, 17)

What is the area outside the circle, but within the square whose two corners are A and B?
    a. $169(1-\pi)$.
    b. 169π.
    c. $169\pi/4$.
    d. $169(1-\pi/4)$.
    e. 169.

7. A line with a slope of 2 passes through the point (2, 4). What is the set of coordinates where that line passes through the y intercept?
    a. (-2, 0).
    b. (0, 0).
    c. (2, 2).
    d. (4, 0).
    e. (1, 1).

8.

$3x + 4y = 7$
$9x + 12y = 21$

Determine where the above two lines intersect:
    a. $x = 4, y = 3$.
    b. $x = 12, y = 9$.
    c. $x = 1/3, y = 1/3$.
    d. Not enough information provided.
    e. There is no solution; the lines do not intersect.

9.

$3x + 4y = 7$
$8x - 6y = 9$

Are the above lines parallel or perpendicular?
    a. Parallel.
    b. Perpendicular.
    c. Neither parallel nor perpendicular.
    d. Cannot be determined.
    e. The angle at the point of intersection is 40.

Absolute Value Equations

1. Factor $x^2 + 2x - 15$.
   a. $(x - 3)(x + 5)$.
   b. $(x + 3)(x - 5)$.
   c. $(x + 3)(x + 5)$.
   d. $(x - 3)(x - 5)$.
   e. $(x - 1)(x + 15)$.

2. Car A starts at 3:15 PM and travels straight to its destination at a constant speed of 50 mph. If it arrives at 4:45 PM, how far did it travel?
   a. 70 miles.
   b. 75 miles.
   c. 65 miles.
   d. 40 miles.
   e. 105 miles.

3. What are the roots of the equation $2x^2 + 14x = 0$?
   a. 0 and 7.
   b. 0 and -7.
   c. 14 and 0.
   d. 2 and 14.
   e. Cannot be determined.

4. If $f(x) = 2x^2 + 3x$, and $g(x) = x + 4$, what is $f[g(x)]$?
   a. $x^2 + 19x + 44$.
   b. $2x^2 + 19x + 44$.
   c. $4x^2 + 35x + 76$.
   d. $x^2 + 8x + 16$.
   e. None of the above.

5. If $|x + 4| = 2$, what are the values of x?
   a. 2 and 6.
   b. -2 and -6.
   c. -2.
   d. -6.
   e. 0.

6. The sale of an item can be written as a function of price: $s = 3p + c$, where s is the amount in sales, p is the price per item, and c is a constant value. If the sales generated are $20 at a price of $5 for the item, then what should the price be to generate $50 in sales?
   a. $10.
   b. $15.
   c. $20.
   d. $16.
   e. $14.

7. If $f(n) = 2n + 3\sqrt{n}$, where n is a positive integer, what is $f[g(5)]$ if $g(m) = m - 4$?
   a. 1.
   b. 2.
   c. 3.
   d. 4.
   e. 5.

8. If $f(x) = (x + 2)^2$, and $-4 \leq x \leq 4$, what is the minimum value of $f(x)$?
   a. 0.
   b. 1.
   c. 2.
   d. 3.
   e. 4.

Geometry

1. What is the area, in square feet, of the triangle whose sides have lengths equal to 3, 4, and 5 feet?
   a. 6 square feet.
   b. 7 square feet.
   c. 4 square feet.
   d. 5 square feet.
   e. 8 square feet.

2. In the following figure, where AE bisects line BC, and angles AEC and AEB are both right angles, what is the length of AB?
   a. 1 cm.
   b. 2 cm.
   c. 3 cm.
   d. 4 cm.
   e. 5 cm.

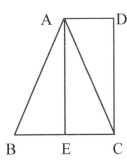

BC = 6 cm
AD − 3 cm
CD = 4 cm

3. In the following triangle, if AB = 6 and BC = 8, what should the length of CA be to make triangle ABC a right triangle?
   a. 10.
   b. 9.
   c. 8.
   d. 4.
   e. 7.

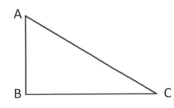

4. In the following circle there is a square with an area of 36 cm². What is the area outside the square, but within the circle?
    a. 18π cm².
    b. 18π - 30 cm².
    c. 18π - 36 cm².
    d. 18 cm².
    e. -18 cm².

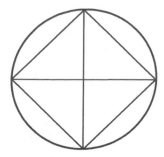

Fundamental Counting Principle, Permutations, Combinations

1. The wardrobe of a studio contains 4 hats, 3 suits, 5 shirts, 2 pants, and 3 pairs of shoes. How many different ways can these items be put together?
    a. 60.
    b. 300.
    c. 360.
    d. 420.
    e. 500.

2. For lunch, you have a choice between chicken fingers or cheese sticks for an appetizer; turkey, chicken, or veal for the main course; cake or pudding for dessert; and either Coke or Pepsi for a beverage. How many choices of possible meals do you have?
    a. 16.
    b. 24.
    c. 34.
    d. 36.
    e. 8.

3. For an office job, I need to pick 3 candidates out of a pool of 5. How many choices do I have?
    a. 60.
    b. 20.
    c. 10.
    d. 30.
    e. 50.

4. A contractor is supposed to choose 3 tiles out of a stack of 5 tiles to make as many patterns as possible. How many different patterns can he make?
    a. 10.
    b. 20.
    c. 30.
    d. 40.
    e. 60.

5. I have chores to do around the house on a weekend. There are 5 chores I must complete by the end of the day. I can choose to do them in any order, so long as they are all completed. How many choices do I have?
    a. 5.
    b. 25.
    c. 32.
    d. 3125.
    e. 120.

Ratios, Proportions, Rate of Change

1. A class has 50% more boys than girls. What is the ratio of boys to girls?
    a. 4:3.
    b. 3:2.
    c. 5:4.
    d. 10:7.
    e. 7:5.

2. A car can travel 30 miles on 4 gallons of gas. If the gas tank has a capacity of 16 gallons, how far can it travel if the tank is ¾ full?
    a. 120 miles.
    b. 90 miles.
    c. 60 miles.
    d. 55 miles.
    e. 65 miles.

3. The profits of a company increase by $5000 every year for five years and then decrease by $2000 for the next two years. What is the average rate of change in the company profit for that seven-year period?
    a. $1000/year.
    b. $2000/year.
    c. $3000/year.
    d. $4000/year.
    e. $5000/year.

4. A bag holds 250 marbles. Of those marbles, 40% are red, 30% are blue, 10% are green, and 20% are black. How many marbles of each color are present in the bag?
    a. Red = 90; Blue = 80; Green = 30; Black = 40.
    b. Red = 80; Blue = 60; Green = 30; Black = 80.
    c. Red = 100; Blue = 75; Green = 25; Black = 50.
    d. Red = 100; Blue = 70; Green = 30; Black = 50.
    e. Red = 120; Blue = 100; Green = 10; Black = 20.

5. Two students from a student body of 30 boys and 50 girls will be selected to serve on the school disciplinary committee. What is the probability that first a boy will be chosen, and then a girl?
    a. 1/1500.
    b. 1500/6400.
    c. 1500/6320.
    d. 1.
    e. 30/50.

Reading Comprehension

Many persons plead a love of truth as an apology for rough manners, as if truth was never gentle and kind, but always harsh, morose, and forbidding. Surely good manners and a good conscience are no more inconsistent with each other than beauty and innocence, which are strikingly akin, and always look the better for companionship. Roughness and honesty are indeed sometimes found together in the same person, but he is a poor judge of human nature who takes ill-manners to be a guarantee of probity of character. Some persons object to politeness, that its language is unmeaning and false. But this is easily answered. A lie is not locked up in a phrase, but must exist, if at all, in the mind of the speaker. In the ordinary compliments of civilized life, there is no intention to deceive, and consequently no falsehood. Polite language is pleasant to the ear, and soothing to the heart, while rough words are just the reverse; and if not the product of ill temper, are very apt to produce it. The plainest of truths, let it be remembered, can be conveyed in civil speech, while the most malignant lies may find utterance, and often do, in the language of the fish market.

1. What is the first sentence in the passage?
    a. Main idea
    b. Topic
    c. Theme
    d. Supporting detail

2. Which is a logical prediction?
    a. The next paragraph will discuss manners at the fish market.
    b. The next paragraph will discuss ways to speak politely.
    c. The next paragraph will discuss table manners.
    d. The next paragraph will discuss how to respond to an invitation.

3. What is the intent?
    a. Persuade
    b. Inform
    c. Entertain
    d. Express feeling

4. Which is an opinion?
    a. Polite language is pleasant to the ear.
    b. Many persons plead a love of truth.
    c. Roughness and honesty are indeed sometimes found together
    d. Some persons object to politeness

I do not mean to prescribe rules to strong and valiant natures, who will mind their own affairs whether in heaven or hell, and perchance build more magnificently and spend more lavishly than the richest, without ever impoverishing themselves, not knowing how they live—if, indeed, there are any such, as has been dreamed; nor to those who find their encouragement and inspiration in precisely the present condition of things, and cherish it with the fondness and enthusiasm of lovers—and, to some extent, I reckon myself in this number; I do not speak to those who are well employed, in whatever circumstances, and they know whether they are well employed or not;—but mainly to the mass of men who are discontented, and idly complaining of the hardness of their lot or of the times, when they might improve them. There are some who complain most energetically and inconsolably of any, because they are, as they say, doing their duty. I also have in my mind that seemingly wealthy, but most terribly impoverished class of all, who have accumulated dross, but know not how to use it, or get rid of it, and thus have forged their own golden or silver fetters.

5. Which is a topic sentence?
    a. There are some who complain most energetically and inconsolably of any, because they are, as they say, doing their duty.
    b. I do not speak to those who are well employed, in whatever circumstances.
    c. I also have in my mind that seemingly wealthy, but most terribly impoverished class of all, who have accumulated dross, but know not how to use it, or get rid of it, and thus have forged their own golden or silver fetters.
    d. I do not mean to prescribe rules to strong and valiant natures, who will mind their own affairs whether in heaven or hell, and perchance build more magnificently and spend more lavishly than the richest, without ever impoverishing themselves, not knowing how they live—if, indeed, there are any such, as has been dreamed; nor to those who find their encouragement and inspiration in precisely the present condition of things, and cherish it with the fondness and enthusiasm of lovers—and, to some extent, I reckon myself in this number; I do not speak to those who are well employed, in whatever circumstances, and they know whether they are well employed or not;—but mainly to the mass of men who are discontented, and idly complaining of the hardness of their lot or of the times, when they might improve them.

6. What is the third sentence in the passage?
    a. Main idea
    b. Topic
    c. Theme
    d. Supporting detail

7. What can be inferred?
    a. The author believes that money is essential for happiness.
    b. The author wants people to find contentment.
    c. The author dislikes wealth.
    d. The author does not believe happiness is possible.

8. Which is a logical conclusion?
    a. The author is going to offer help finding new, meaningful employment.
    b. The author is going to recommend saving money, rather than spending.
    c. The author is going to suggest a path to contentment.
    d. The author is going to suggest that people give away their money.

9. What is the main purpose?
    a. To explain why wealth causes unhappiness
    b. To explain why wealth causes happiness
    c. To differentiate to whom the author is speaking
    d. To tell the reader the topic of the essay

10. Which type of passage is this?
    a. Narrative
    b. Expository
    c. Technical
    d. Persuasive

11. Which is a summary sentence?
    a. The wealthy spend lavishly.
    b. New money causes unhappiness.
    c. Hard work will bring happiness.
    d. Happiness and contentment is largely a matter of attitude and personality, rather than wealth.

I did not, when a slave, understand the deep meaning of those rude and apparently incoherent songs. I was myself within the circle; so that I neither saw nor heard as those without might see and hear. They told a tale of woe which was then altogether beyond my feeble comprehension; they were tones loud, long, and deep; they breathed the prayer and complaint of souls boiling over with the bitterest anguish. Every tone was a testimony against slavery, and a prayer to God for deliverance from chains. The hearing of those wild notes always depressed my spirit, and filled me with ineffable sadness. I have frequently found myself in tears while hearing them. The mere recurrence to those songs, even now, afflicts me; and while I am writing these lines, an expression of feeling has already found its way down my cheek. To those songs I trace my first glimmering conception of the dehumanizing character of slavery. I can never get rid of that conception. Those songs still follow me, to deepen my hatred of slavery, and quicken my sympathies for my brethren in bonds. If any one wishes to be impressed with the soul-killing effects of slavery, let him go to Colonel Lloyd's plantation, and, on allowance-day, place himself in the deep pine woods, and there let him, in silence, analyze the sounds that shall pass through the chambers of his soul,—and if he is not thus impressed, it will only be because "there is no flesh in his obdurate heart."

12. Which is a logical conclusion?
    a. The narrator was once a slave.
    b. The narrator is still a slave.
    c. This is a work of fiction.
    d. Colonel Lloyd is the narrator.

13. Which type of passage is this?
    a. Narrative
    b. Expository
    c. Technical
    d. Persuasive writing

14. What is the main purpose?
    a. To explain the history of slave music
    b. To convince the reader to abolish slavery
    c. To share a personal story
    d. To explain why Colonel Lloyd was unkind

Regardless of the time of the year or the time of the day there are pies. The Pennsylvania Dutch eat pies for breakfast. They eat pies for lunch. They eat pies for dinner and they eat pies for midnight snacks. Pies are made with a great variety of ingredients from the apple pie we all know to the rivel pie which is made from flour, sugar, and butter. The Dutch housewife is as generous with her pies as she is with all her cooking, baking six or eight at a time not one and two.

The apple is an important Pennsylvania Dutch food. Dried apples form the basis for many typical dishes. Each fall barrels of apples are converted into cider. Apple butter is one of the Pennsylvania Dutch foods which has found national acceptance. The making of apple butter is an all-day affair and has the air of a holiday to it. Early in the morning the neighbors gather and begin to peel huge piles of apples that will be needed. Soon the great copper apple butter kettle is brought out and set up over a wood fire. Apple butter requires constant stirring to prevent burning. However, stirring can be light work for a boy and a girl when they're young and the day is bright and the world is full of promise. By dusk the apple butter is made, neighborhood news is brought up to date and hunger has been driven that much further away for the coming winter.

Food is abundant and appetites are hearty in the Pennsylvania Dutch country. The traditional dishes are relatively simple and unlike most regional cookery the ingredients are readily available. Best of all, no matter who makes them the results are "wonderful good."

15. Which is a logical conclusion?
    a. Pennsylvania Dutch housewives like to cook.
    b. Pie is the only food they eat.
    c. Food is an important part of Pennsylvania Dutch culture.
    d. Apple butter is used to make pies.

16. Which is a logical conclusion?
    a. Apples are a significant crop in Pennsylvania Dutch country.
    b. Pies require only butter, sugar and flour.
    c. Apple butter is made in the spring.
    d. Pennsylvania Dutch children all learn to cook.

17. Which is an opinion?
    a. Pennsylvania Dutch housewives frequently make pie.
    b. Pennsylvania Dutch children help make apple butter.
    c. Pennsylvania Dutch food is "wonderful good".
    d. Apple butter takes all day to make.

18. Which type of passage is this?
    a. Narrative
    b. Expository
    c. Technical
    d. Persuasive

19. What can be inferred?
    a. This is the introduction to a cookbook.
    b. This is the beginning of a history book.
    c. This is a book about Pennsylvania Dutch culture.
    d. This is a book about regional foods.

20. What is the first sentence in the passage?
    a. Main idea
    b. Topic
    c. Theme
    d. Supporting detail

I don't know whether you have ever seen a map of a person's mind. Doctors sometimes draw maps of other parts of you, and your own map can become intensely interesting, but catch them trying to draw a map of a child's mind, which is not only confused, but keeps going round all the time. There are zigzag lines on it, just like your temperature on a card, and these are probably roads in the island, for the Neverland is always more or less an island, with astonishing splashes of colour here and there, and coral reefs and rakish-looking craft in the offing, and savages and lonely lairs, and gnomes who are mostly tailors, and caves through which a river runs, and princes with six elder brothers, and a hut fast going to decay, and one very small old lady with a hooked nose. It would be an easy map if that were all, but there is also first day at school, religion, fathers, the round pond, needle-work, murders, hangings, verbs that take the dative, chocolate pudding day, getting into braces, say ninety-nine, three-pence for pulling out your tooth yourself, and so on, and either these are part of the island or they are another map showing through, and it is all rather confusing, especially as nothing will stand still.

21. What is the intent?
    a. Persuade
    b. Entertain
    c. Inform
    d. Express feeling

22. Which is a topic sentence?
    a. I don't know whether you have ever seen a map of a person's mind.
    b. Doctors sometimes draw maps of other parts of you, but catch them trying to draw a map of a child's mind, which is not only confused but keeps going round all the time.
    c. There are zigzag lines on it, just like your temperature on a card, and these are probably roads in the island.
    d. It would be an easy map if that were all, but there is also first day at school, religion, fathers, the round pond.

23. What can be inferred?
    a. The child's mind is being compared to Neverland.
    b. Neverland is an island.
    c. There are maps of Neverland.
    d. Neverland has chocolate pudding.

24. Which type of passage is this?
    a. Narrative
    b. Expository
    c. Persuasive
    d. Technical

Malvern Hill, a plateau a mile and a half long and half a mile wide, with its top bare of woods, commanded a view of the country over which the Confederates must approach. Around the summit of this hill McClellan had placed tier after tier of batteries, arranged like an amphitheater. On the top were placed several heavy siege guns, his left flank being protected by the gunboats in the river. The morning and early afternoon were occupied by several Confederate attacks, sometimes formidable in their nature, but Lee planned for no general move until he could bring up a force which he thought sufficient to attack the strong position of the Federals. The Confederates had orders to advance, when a signal shout was given by the men of Armistead's brigade. The attack was made late in the afternoon by General D. H. Hill, and was gallantly done, but no army could have withstood the fire from the batteries of McClellan as they were massed upon Malvern Hill. All during the evening brigade after brigade tried to force the Union lines. They were forced to breast one of the most devastating storms of lead and canister to which an assaulting army has ever been subjected. The round shot and grape cut through the branches of the trees. Column after column of Southern soldiers rushed upon the death dealing cannon, only to be mowed down. Their thin lines rallied again and again to the charge, but to no avail. McClellan's batteries still hurled their missiles of death. The field below was covered with the dead, as mute pleaders in the cause of peace. The heavy shells from the gunboats on the river shrieked through the timber and great limbs were torn from the trees as they hurtled by. Darkness was falling over the combatants. It was nine o'clock before the guns ceased firing, and only an occasional shot rang out over the gory field of Malvern Hill.

25. What is the intent?
    a. Persuade
    b. Entertain
    c. Inform
    d. Express feeling

26. Which is a likely motive for the author?
    a. To provide historical information
    b. To share opinions about the war
    c. To explain why the war ended slavery
    d. To persuade the reader that war was wrong

27. Which is a summary sentence?
    a. The Battle of Malvern Hill was a decisive Confederate victory.
    b. The Battle of Malvern Hill was a decisive Union victory.
    c. The Battle of Malvern Hill was a part of the Revolutionary war.
    d. The hill offered the Confederates a better position in the battle.

28. Which type of passage is this?
    a. Narrative
    b. Expository
    c. Technical
    d. Persuasive

29. Which accurately represents the historical context of the information in the passage?
    a. World War I
    b. The Civil War
    c. World War II
    d. The Revolutionary War

30. What can be inferred?
    a. This is part of a book about the Civil War
    b. This is a memoir of a Confederate soldier
    c. This is a memoir of a Union soldier
    d. This is a biography of a Confederate general

Many persons plead a love of truth as an apology for rough manners, as if truth was never gentle and kind, but always harsh, morose, and forbidding. Surely good manners and a good conscience are no more inconsistent with each other than beauty and innocence, which are strikingly akin, and always look the better for companionship. Roughness and honesty are indeed sometimes found together in the same person, but he is a poor judge of human nature who takes ill-manners to be a guarantee of probity of character. Some persons object to politeness, that its language is unmeaning and false. But this is easily answered. A lie is not locked up in a phrase, but must exist, if at all, in the mind of the speaker. In the ordinary compliments of civilized life, there is no intention to deceive, and consequently no falsehood. Polite language is pleasant to the ear, and soothing to the heart, while rough words are just the reverse; and if not the product of ill temper, are very apt to produce it. The plainest of truths, let it be remembered, can be conveyed in civil speech, while the most malignant lies may find utterance, and often do, in the language of the fish market.

31. What is the main idea of the passage?
    a. Fishmongers have bad manners.
    b. Good manners and honesty can go together.
    c. A little white lie is necessary for politeness.
    d. Poor manners are not a sign of honesty.

32. Which statement is not a detail from the passage?
    a. Truth can be gentle and kind.
    b. Honesty is often an excuse for bad manners.
    c. Lies can be conveyed with rough manners.
    d. People with good manners intend to deceive.

33. What is the meaning of <u>deceive</u> near the end of the paragraph?
    a. Make someone believe something that is not true
    b. Convince someone to give you something
    c. Spread an unkind story about someone else
    d. Share truths or speak honestly

34. What is the author's primary purpose in writing this passage?
    a. To emphasize the importance of honesty
    b. To share information about fish markets
    c. To talk about the differences in manners among the social classes
    d. To explain that manners and honesty can coexist

35. Which is the best summary of this passage?
    a. Civil speech helps people to get along.
    b. Honesty is always the best policy.
    c. Good manners help you to lie.
    d. Rough manners cause fights.

"However, let us go to dinner, and I will soon tell you whether you are a well-bred man or not; and here let me premise that what is good manners for a small dinner is good manners for a large one, and vice versâ. Now, the first thing you do is to sit down. Stop, sir! Pray do not cram yourself into the table in that way; no, nor sit a yard from it, like that. How graceless, inconvenient, and in the way of conversation! Why, dear me! You are positively putting your elbows on the table, and now you have got your hands fumbling about with the spoons and forks, and now you are nearly knocking my new hock glasses over. Can't you take your hands down, sir? Didn't you learn that in the nursery? Didn't your mamma say to you, 'Never put your hands above the table except to carve or eat?' Oh! But come, no nonsense, sit up, if you please. I can't have your fine head of hair forming a side dish on my table; you must not bury your face in the plate, you came to show it, and it ought to be alive. Well, but there is no occasion to throw your head back like that, you look like an alderman, sir, after dinner. Pray, don't lounge in that sleepy way. You are here to eat, drink, and be merry. You can sleep when you get home.

36. What is the main idea of the passage?
    a. Aldermen drink too much.
    b. Well-bred individuals have good manners.
    c. You should not nap at the dinner table.
    d. Don't put your hands above the table.

37. Which statement is not a detail from the passage?
    a. Don't put your hands above the table.
    b. Don't sit a yard from the table.
    c. Don't lean over your plate.
    d. Don't put your elbows on the table.

38. What is the meaning of <u>lounge</u> near the end of the paragraph?
    a. Couch or sofa
    b. Lay down
    c. Sleep
    d. Relax

39. What is the author's primary purpose in writing this passage?
    a. To teach manners.
    b. To amuse the reader.
    c. To explain why you should not go to dinner parties.
    d. To illustrate how to properly eat fish.

40. Which is the best summary of this passage?
    a. Good manners are common sense.
    b. Use good manners at meals.
    c. No one has good manners.
    d. Good manners are unimportant

Writing

Questions 1 – 5 are based on the following original passage. Sentences are numbered at the end for easy reference within the questions.

Examining the impact my lifestyle has on the earth's resources is, I believe, a fascinating and valuable thing to do (1). According to the Earth Day Network ecological footprint calculator, it would take four planet earths to sustain the human population if everyone used as many resources as I do (2). My "ecological footprint," or the amount of productive area of the earth that is required to produce the resources I consume, is therefore larger than the footprints of most of the population (3). It is hard to balance the luxuries and opportunities I have available to me with doing what I know to be better from an ecological standpoint (4).

It is fairly easy for me to recycle, so I do it, but it would be much harder to forgo the opportunity to travel by plane or eat my favorite fruits that have been flown to the supermarket from a different country (5). Although I get ecological points for my recycling habits, my use of public transportation, and living in an apartment complex rather than a free-standing residence, <u>my footprint expands when it is taken into account my not-entirely-local diet</u>, my occasional use of a car, my three magazine subscriptions, and my history of flying more than ten hours a year (6). I feel that realizing just how unfair my share of the earth's resources have been should help me to change at least some of my bad habits (7).

1. Which of the following is the best version of sentence 1?
    a. It is fascinating and valuable to examine the impact that my lifestyle has on the earth's resources.
    b. Examining the impact my lifestyle has on the earth's resources is a fascinating and valuable thing to do.
    c. To examine the impact my lifestyle has on the earth's resources is fascinating and is also valuable.
    d. The impact of my lifestyle on the earth's resources is fascinating and valuable to examine.
    e. Examining the impact my lifestyle has on the earth's resources is, I believe, a fascinating and valuable thing to do.

2. How could sentences 2 and 3 best be combined?
    a. According to the Earth Day Network ecological footprint calculator, it would take four planet earths to sustain the human population if everyone used as many resources as I do because I have a very large "ecological footprint," which is the amount of productive area of the earth that is required to produce the resources I consume.
    b. According to the Earth Day Network ecological footprint calculator, which calculates the amount of productive area of the earth that is required to produce the resources one consumes, it would take four planet earths to sustain the human population if everyone had a footprint as large as mine.
    c. According to the Earth Day Network ecological footprint calculator, it would take four planet earths to sustain the human population if everyone used as many resources as I do; my "ecological footprint," or the amount of productive area of the earth that is required to produce the resources I consume, is therefore larger than the footprints of most of the population.
    d. According to the Earth Day Network ecological footprint calculator, which measures the amount of productive area of the earth that is required to produce the resources a person consumes, my footprint is larger than that of most; it would take four planet earths to sustain the human population if everyone consumed as much as I do.
    e. According to the Earth Day Network ecological footprint calculator, my "ecological footprint," or the amount of productive area of the earth that is required to produce the resources I consume, would require four planet earths if it were to be the footprint of the human population; it is therefore larger than the footprints of most of the population.

3. Sentence 4 would best fit if it were moved where in this composition?
    a. At the beginning of paragraph 2.
    b. After sentence 5.
    c. After sentence 6.
    d. At the end of paragraph 2.
    e. Sentence 4 is best left where it is.

4. Which two sentences would be improved by switching positions?
    a. 1 and 2.
    b. 3 and 4.
    c. 5 and 6.
    d. 6 and 7.
    e. 2 and 7.

5. Which of the following should replace the underlined portion of sentence 6?
    a. "my footprint expands when taken into account my not-entirely-local diet"
    b. "my footprint expands when taken into account are my not-entirely-local diet"
    c. "my footprint expands when we take into account my not-entirely-local diet"
    d. "my footprint expands when one takes into account my not-entirely-local diet"
    e. "my footprint expands when it is taken into account my not-entirely-local diet"

6. Which revision would most improve sentence 7?
   a. Eliminate the phrase "I feel that."
   b. Change "should help me" to "will help me."
   c. Add the phrase "In conclusion," to the beginning.
   d. Change "have been" to "has been."
   e. Eliminate the phrase "at least some of."

Questions 7 – 12 are based on the short passage below, which is excerpted from Thomas Huxley's preface to his Collected Essays: Volume V (public domain) and modified slightly. Sentences are numbered at the end for easy reference within the questions.

I had set out on a journey, with no other purpose than that of exploring a certain province of natural knowledge, I strayed no hair's breadth from the course which it was my right and my duty to pursue; and yet I found that, whatever route I took, before long, I came to a tall and formidable-looking fence (1). Confident I might be in the existence of an ancient and indefeasible right of way, before me stood the thorny barrier with its comminatory notice-board—"No Thoroughfare. By order" (2). There seemed no way over; nor did the prospect of creeping round, as I saw some do, attracts me (3). True there was no longer any cause to fear the spring guns and man-traps set by former lords of the manor; but one is apt to get very dirty going on all-fours (4). The only alternatives were either to give up my journey—which I was not minded to do—or to break the fence down and go through it (5). I swiftly ruled out crawling under as an option (6). I also ruled out turning back (7).

7. How could sentence 1 best be changed?
   a. The comma after journey should be removed.
   b. The comma after knowledge should be changed to a semicolon.
   c. "and yet" should be eliminated.
   d. Change "I had set out" to "I set out."
   e. No change.

8. Sentence 6 should be placed where in the passage?
   a. After sentence 1.
   b. After sentence 2.
   c. After sentence 3.
   d. After sentence 4.
   e. Left after sentence 5.

9. Which edit should be made in sentence 3?
   a. "nor" should be changed to "or."
   b. "seemed" should be changed to "seems."
   c. "me" should be changed to "I."
   d. "attracts" should be changed to "attract."
   e. No edit should be made.

10. How could sentences 6 and 7 best be combined?
    a. Swiftly, I ruled out crawling under as an option and also turning back.
    b. Ruling out two options swiftly: crawling under and turning back.
    c. I swiftly ruled out the options of crawling under or turning back.
    d. I ruled out crawling under as an option and I swiftly also ruled out turning back.
    e. I swiftly ruled out crawling under as an option and also turning back.

11. Which word could be inserted at the beginning of sentence 2 before "confident" to best clarify the meaning?
   a. Even.
   b. However.
   c. Hardly.
   d. Finally.
   e. Especially.

12. Which of the following is the best way to split sentence 1 into two separate sentences?
   a. I had set out on a journey, with no other purpose than that of exploring a certain province of natural knowledge. I strayed no hair's breadth from the course which it was my right and my duty to pursue; and yet I found that, whatever route I took, before long, I came to a tall and formidable-looking fence.
   b. I had set out on a journey, with no other purpose than that of exploring a certain province of natural knowledge, I strayed no hair's breadth from the course which it was my right and my duty to pursue. Yet I found that, whatever route I took, before long, I came to a tall and formidable-looking fence.
   c. I had set out on a journey, with no other purpose than that of exploring a certain province of natural knowledge, I strayed no hair's breadth from the course which it was my right and my duty to pursue; and yet I found that, whatever route I took, before long. I came to a tall and formidable-looking fence.
   d. I had set out on a journey. With no other purpose than that of exploring a certain province of natural knowledge, I strayed no hair's breadth from the course which it was my right and my duty to pursue; and yet I found that, whatever route I took, before long, I came to a tall and formidable-looking fence.
   e. I had set out on a journey, with no other purpose than that of exploring a certain province of natural knowledge, I strayed no hair's breadth from the course which it was my right and my duty to pursue; and yet. I found that, whatever route I took, before long, I came to a tall and formidable-looking fence.

Questions 13 – 27 are based on the short passage below:

[1]Sandra Cisneros, perhaps the best known Latina author in the United States, writes poems and stories whose titles alone – "Barbie-Q," "My Lucy Friend Who Smells Like Corn," "Woman Hollering Creek" – engage potential readers' curiosity. [2]Ironically, this renowned writer, whose books are printed on recycled paper, did not do wellin school. [3]When she lectures at schools and public libraries, Cisneros presents the evidence. [4]An elementary school report card containing Cs, Ds and a solitary B (for conduct). [5]Cisneros has a theory to explain her low grades: teachers had low expectations for Latina and Latino students from Chicago's South Side. [6]Despite the obstacles that she faced in school, Cisneros completed not only high school but also college. [7]Her persistence paid off in her twenties, when Cisneros was admitted <u>prestigious</u> to the Writers' Workshop at the University of Iowa.

[8]Cisneros <u>soon</u> observed that most of her classmates at the university seemed to have a common set of memories, based on middle-class childhoods, from which to draw in their writing. [9]Cisneros felt <u>decided</u> out of place. _____("9A")_____. [10]She decided to speak from her own experience. [11]Her voice, which by being one of a Latina living outside of the mainstream, found a large and attentive audience in 1984 with the publication of her first short story collection, The House on Mango Street. [12]<u>Today</u> the book is read by middle school, high school, and college students across the United States. [13]Cisneros uses her influence as a successful writer to help other Latina and Latino writers get their works published. [14]But <u>having made the argument that</u>, in order for large numbers of young Latinos to achieve literary success, the educational system itself must change. [15]Cisneros <u>hints</u> that she succeeded in spite of the educational system. "I'm the exception," she insists, "not the rule."

13. What change should be made to sentence 1?
    a. No Change.
    b. "author and writer."
    c. "author and novelist."
    d. "wordsmith and author."

14. What change should be made towards the end of sentence 1?
    a. No Change.
    b. "potential, reader's."
    c. "potential, readers."
    d. "potential readers."

15. What change should be made to sentence 2?
    a. No Change.
    b. "writer, who is recognized by her orange and black eyeglasses"
    c. "writer, who likes to write at night,"
    d. "writer"

16. What change should be made to sentence 3?
    a. No Change.
    b. "evidence: an"
    c. "evidence; an"
    d. "evidence an"

17. The best placement for the underlined portion in sentence 7 would be:
    a. Where it is now.
    b. Before the word admitted.
    c. Before the word "Writers'."
    d. Before the word "Workshop."

18. Which word would best replace the underlined portion in sentence 8?
    a. No Change.
    b. "furthermore"
    c. "nevertheless"
    d. "therefore"

19. Which of the following is the best beginning of sentence 9?
    a. No Change.
    b. "Cisneros herself,"
    c. "Cisneros, herself"
    d. "Cisneros,"

20. Which of the following should replace the underlined word in sentence 9?
    a. No Change.
    b. "deciding"
    c. "decidedly"
    d. "decidedly and"

21. Which of the following true statements, if added at _____("9A")_____ , would best serve as a transition between the challenges Cisneros faced as an aspiring writer and her success in meeting those challenges?
    a. "She did not know what to do."
    b. "Then she had a break through."
    c. "At that point she almost went home to Chicago."
    d. "She wondered whether she was in the right field."

22. Which of the following changes should be made to sentence 11?
    a. No Change.
    b. "voice – that of a Latina living outside the mainstream –"
    c. "voice, being one of a Latina living outside the mainstream, it"
    d. "voice – in which it was a Latina living outside the mainstream –"

23. Which of the following changes should be made to sentence 11?
    a. No Change.
    b. "1984, With"
    c. "1984; with"
    d. "1984, with,"

24. Which of the following is the best change to the underlined word at the beginning of sentence 12?
    a. No Change.
    b. "In the future,"
    c. "Meanwhile,"
    d. "At the same time,"

25. Which of the following is the best replacement for the underlined portion in sentence 14?
    a. No Change.
    b. "she argues that,"
    c. "arguing that,"
    d. "she argues that, when"

26. Which choice best shows that Cisneros is emphatic about expressing the belief stated in the underlined portion of sentence 15?
    a. No Change.
    b. "Says."
    c. "Supposes."
    d. "Asserts."

27. The writer is considering deleting the last sentence. If the writer decided to delete this sentence, the paragraph would primarily lose a statement that:
    a. Enhances the subject and setting.
    b. Provides support for a point previously made.
    c. Humorously digresses from the main topic of the paragraph.
    d. Contradicts Cisneros's claim made earlier in the essay.

Questions 28-40 are based on the short passage below:

[1]Traveling on commercial airlines has changed substantially <u>over years</u>. [2]When commercial air travel first became available, it was so expensive that usually only businessmen could afford <u>to do so</u>. [3]Airplane efficiency, the relative cost of fossil fuels, <u>and using economies</u> of scale have all contributed to make travel by air more affordable and common. [4]These days, there are nearly 30,000 commercial air flights in the world each day!

[5]Depending on the size of the airport you are departing from, you should arrive 90 minutes to two and a half hours before your plane leaves. [6]Things like checking your luggage and flying internationally can make the process of getting to your gate take longer. [7]If you fly out of a very busy airport, like <u>LaGuardia, in</u> New York City, on a very busy travel day, like the day before Thanksgiving, you can easily miss your flight if you don't arrive early enough.

[8]Security processes for passengers have also changed. In the 1960s, there was <u>hardly any</u> security: you could just buy your ticket and walk on to the plane the day of the flight without even needing to show identification. [9]In the 1970s, American commercial airlines started installing sky marshals on many <u>flights, an</u> undercover law enforcement officers who would protect the passengers from a potential hijacking.

[10]Also in the early 1970s, the federal government began to require that airlines screen passengers and their luggage for things like weapons and bombs. [11]After the 2001 terrorist attacks in the United States, these requirements were <u>stringently enforced</u>. [12]Family members can no longer meet someone at the <u>gate; only ticketed passengers are allowed into the gate area</u>. [13]The definition of <u>weapons are</u> not allowed is expanded every time there is a new incident for example liquids are now restricted on planes after an attempted planned attack using gel explosives in 2006.

[14]Despite the hassles of traveling by air, it is still a boon to modern <u>life.</u> [14]<u>Still, some</u> businesses are moving away from sending employees on airplane trips, <u>as</u> face-to-face video conferencing technologies improve. [15]A trip which might take ten hours by car <u>can take only</u> two hours by plane. [16]However, the ability to travel quickly by air <u>will always be valued, by citizens</u> of our modern society.

28. Which of the following is the best change to the underlined portion of sentence 1?
   a. No Change.
   b. "over the years"
   c. "over time"
   d. Delete.

29. Which of the following is the best change to the underlined portion of sentence 2?
   a. No Change.
   b. "to do it"
   c. "to fly"
   d. "do so"

30. Which of the following is the best change to the underlined portion of sentence 3?
   a. No Change.
   b. "using economies"
   c. "and the use of economies"
   d. "and economies"

31. Which of the following is the best change to the underlined portion of sentence 7?
   a. No Change.
   b. "La Guardia in"
   c. "La Guardia; in"
   d. "La Guardia,"

32. Which of the following is the best change to the underlined portion of sentence 7?
   a. No Change.
   b. "hardly"
   c. "no"
   d. "barely'

33. Which of the following is the best change to the underlined portion of sentence 9?
   a. No Change.
   b. "flights; an"
   c. "flights. Marshals arc"
   d. "flights, marshals are"

34. Which of the following is the best change to the underlined portion of sentence 11?
   a. No Change.
   b. "stiffly upheld"
   c. "enforced with more stringency"
   d. "more stringently enforced"

35. If the underlined portion in sentence 12 were deleted, the passage would lose:
   a. No Change.
   b. An explanation of the screening process.
   c. Ambiguity over why family members are no longer allowed at the gate.
   d. A further specific example of how regulations have changed over time.

36. Which of the following is the best change to the underlined portion in sentence 13?
    a. No Change.
    b. "weapon is"
    c. "weapons"
    d. "weapons which are"

37. Which of the following is the proper transition between sentences 13 & 14?
    a. No Change.
    b. "life. Some"
    c. "life even though some"
    d. "life, still some"

38. Which of the following is the best replacement for the underlined word in sentence 14?
    a. No Change.
    b. "because"
    c. "while"
    d. "since"

39. Which of the following is the best change to the underlined portion in sentence 15?
    a. No Change.
    b. "may only take"
    c. "takes only"
    d. "will only take"

40. Which of the following is the best change to the underlined portion in sentence 16?
    a. No Change.
    b. "citizens will always value"
    c. "will always, be valued by citizens"
    d. "will always be valued by citizens"

Use the prompt below to answer Question 41.

41. Write an essay in 25 minutes by answering the question from your perspective. Be sure to provide evidence.

   • *General George S. Patton Jr. is quoted as having said, "No good decision was ever made in a swivel chair."*

   Is it necessary to be directly in a situation in order to best understand what must be done?

Practice Test 1—Answers

Mathematics

Percent/Part/Whole, Percent

1. **e.**
   The entire class has 42 students, 18 of which are boys, meaning 42 - 18 = 24 is the number of girls. Out of these 24 girls, 2 leave; so 22 girls are left. The total number of students is now 42 - 2 = 40.

   $22/40 * 100 = 55\%$.

   Reminder: If you forget to subtract 2 from the total number of students, you will end up with 60% as the answer. Sometimes you may calculate an answer that has been given as a choice; it can still be incorrect. Always check your answer.

2. **b.**
   If out of the entire paycheck, 20% is first taken out, then the remainder is 80%. Of this remainder, if 30% is used for entertainment, then $(.8 - .80 * .30) = .560$ is left. If 10% is put into a retirement account, then $(.56 - .56 * .1) = .504$ is remaining. So out of $500, the part that remains is 50%, which is $252.

3. **d.**
   In 2005, the value was 1.8 times its value in 1995. So $1.8x = 7200 \rightarrow x = 4000$.

4. **c.**
   $60 * (100 - 25)/100 \rightarrow 60 * .75 = 45$.

5. **b.**
   New price = original price $* (1 - \text{discount}) \rightarrow$ new price $= 70(1-.3) = 49$.

Mean, Median, Mode

1. **d.**
   If test A avg = 21 for 5 tests, then sum of test A results = 21 * 5 = 105.
   If test B avg = 23 for 13 tests, then sum of test B results = 23 * 13 = 299.
   So total result = 299 + 105 = 404.
   Average of all tests = 404/(5 + 13) = 404/18 = 22.44.

2. **b.**
   The average of the first 6 points is 12 $\rightarrow s_1/6 = 12 \rightarrow s_1 = 72$; s_1 is the sum of the first 6 points.

   The average of the next 2 points is 20 $\rightarrow s_2/2 = 20 \rightarrow s_2 = 40$; s_2 is the sum of the next 2 points.

   The average of the remaining 4 points is 4 $\rightarrow s_3/4 = 4 \rightarrow s_3 = 16$; s_3 is the sum of the last 4 points.

   The sum of all the data points = 72 + 40 + 16 = 128.

The average $= 128/12 = 10.67$.

3. **e.**
   Average $= (3 * 55 + 2 * 35 + 3 * 70)/8$ → Average $= 55.625$.

4. **c.**
   Average of high $s = (80 + 95 + 78 + 79 + 94 + 67 + 76)/7 = 81.29$.

   Average of low $s = (45 + 34 + 47 + 55 + 35 + 46 + 54)/7 = 45.14$.

Exponents and Roots

1. **c.**
   $x^2y^3z^5/y^2z^{-9} = x^2y^3z^5 * y^{-2}z^9$ which gives the answer $x^2y^{(3-2)}z^{(5+9)}$ → x^2yz^{14}.

2. **d.**
   Expand $(2m^3)^5$ to give $32m^{15}$.

   So $32m^{15} = 32m^{k+1}$ → $k+1 = 15$ → $k = 14$.

3. **d.**
   $x^5y^4z^3/x^{-3}y^2z^{-4} = x^5y^4z^3 * x^3y^{-2}z^4 = x^8y^2z^7$.

Algebraic Equations

1. **d.**
   If the number is divisible by 2, d should be even. If the number is divisible by 5, then b has to equal 0.

   Start by making both variables 0 and dividing by the largest factor, 7.

   $56800/7 = 8114$.

   2 from 56800 is 56798, a number divisible by 2 and 7.

   Next add a multiple of 7 that turns the last number to a 0. $6 * 7 = 42$. $56798 + 42 = 56840$, which is divisible by 2, 5, and 7.

2. **c.**
   Carla's age is c; Megan's age is m. $c = 3m$; $c - 8 = m - 8 + 18$.

   Substitute $3m$ for c in equation 2 → $3m - 8 = m + 10$ → $m = 9$.

3. **e.**
   We know $(x^2 - 25) = (x + 5)(x - 5)$.

   So $(x^2 - 25)/(x + 5) = x - 5$. At $x = 0$, $f(0) = -5$.

4. **b.**

   Let j be John's age and s be Sally's age.

   $j + 4 = 2(s + 4)$.

   $s - 8 = 10 \rightarrow s = 18$.

   So $j + 4 = 2(18 + 4) \rightarrow j = 40$.

5. **a.**

   If x is the number of marbles initially, then $.25x$ goes to Vic, $.2x$ goes to Robbie, and $.1x$ goes to Jules.

   The number left, x, is $(1 - .25 - .2 - .1) = .45x$.

   Of that I give 6/20 to my brother, so $6/20 * .45x$.

   I am left with $.45x(1 - (6/20)) = .315x$.

   We are also told $.315x = 315 \rightarrow x = 1000$.

6. **c.**

   Always read the question carefully! Questions 5 and 6 are similar, but they are not the same.

   Let x be the original number of marbles. After Vic's share is given $.75x$ remains. After Robbie's share $.75x * .80$ remains. After Jules' share, $.75x * .8 * .9$ remains.

   After I give my brother his share, $.75x * .8 * .9 * (1 - 6/20)$ remains. The remaining number $= .378x$.

   We are told $.378x = 315 \rightarrow x = 833.33$. We need to increase this to the next highest number, 834, because we have part of a marble and to include it we need to have a whole marble.

7. **c.**

   Replace the value of x with its value and solve the equation.

   $29 = 5y + 4$.

   Solving:

   $29 - 4 = 5y + 4 - 4$.

   $25 = 5y$ or $5y = 25$.

   $5y/5 = 25/5$.

   $y = 5$.

8. **b.**

$2(8) + x > 45$ means $x > 29$, so we need more than 29 marbles. A bag has 8 marbles, so the number of bags needed is 29/8, or 3.625. Since we need 3 bags + part of another bag, we need 4 additional bags to give at least 45 marbles.

9. **b.**

n is the number of widgets. The cost the factory incurs for making n widgets is $10000 + 50n$. The amount the factory makes by selling n widgets is $550n$.

At the break-even point, the cost incurred is equal to the amount of sales.

$10000 + 50n = 550n$ → $n = 20$.

Inequalities, Literal Equations, Polynomials, and Binomials

1. **a.**
Choice **a)** will always be true, while the other choices can never be true.

2. **b.**
$25x^2 - 40x + 32 < 22$ → $25x^2 - 40x + 16 < 6$ → $(5x - 4)^2 < 6$ → $5x - 4 < 6$.

$x = 2$, so x has to be all numbers less than 2 for this inequality to work.

3. **c.**
Rearrange equation $x > 6 + 2y$, so $2 > 6 + 2y$. Solve for y.

$2 \geq 6 + 2y$.

$-4 \geq 2y$, so $-2 \leq y$ or $y \geq -2$.

(When working with inequalities, remember to reverse the sign when dividing by a negative number.)

4. **b.**
Find the slopes first. If they are not equal, then the lines intersect. The slopes are -1/2 and 3.

Next, solve by substitution or addition. From the first equation, $x = 4 - 2y$. Plugging this into equation 2, we get $3(4 - 2y) - y = 26$ → $7y = 12 - 26$ → $y = -2$. Plug this value into either equation to find x.

With equation 1, we get $x - 4 = 4$ → $x = 8$.

5. **c.**
Add the equations to eliminate b. $2a = 6$ → $a = 3$.

6. **a.**
Square both equations.

Equation 1 becomes $a + 2\sqrt{ab} + b = 4$; and equation 2 becomes $a - 2\sqrt{ab} + b = 9$.

Add the equations.
$2(a + b) = 13 \rightarrow a + b = 13/2.$ $13/2 = 6.5.$

Slope and Distance to Midpoint

1. **d.**
   The standard form of the line equation is $y = mx + b$. We need to find slope m.

   $m = (y_2 - y_1)/(x_2 - x_1) \rightarrow m = (5 - 8)/(3 - 0) \rightarrow m = -1.$

   Therefore the equation is $y = -x + 8$.

2. **a.**
   At $x = 3$, $((3 * 3) - 4)^2 = 4y - 15$.

   $(9 - 4)^2 = 4y - 15.$

   $25 = 4y - 15.$

   $40 = 4y.$

   $y = 10.$

3. **d.**
   Rearrange the equation and combine like terms. $-5y = 4x$.

   At $x = -10$, $y = 8$. At $x = 5$, $y = -4$. The range of y is therefore $-4 \leq y < 8$.

4. **e.**
   If Judy gets x dollars, then Jennifer gets $3x$ in a week. In a month, Jennifer will then get $4 * 3x$.

   If Judy gets $5 per week, then Jennifer gets $60 in a month.

5. **d.**
   Combine like terms.

   $5x + 9y = 3x - 6y + 5 \rightarrow 2x = -15y + 5 \rightarrow x = -57.5$ when $y = 8$.

6. **d.**
   First we need to find the length of side AB.

   $AB = \sqrt{(17 - 5)^2 + (8 - 3)^2} = 13.$

   If $AB = 13$, then $A_{square} = 13^2 = 169$.

   AB is also the diameter of the circle. $A_{circle} \pi (d^2/4) = 169 \pi /4$.

   The area outside the circle and within the square is: $A_{square} - A_{circle} = 169(1 - \pi /4)$.

7. **b.**
   The slope of the line is given as $m = (y_2 - y_1)/(x_2 - x_1)$, where (x_1, y_1) and (x_2, y_2) are two points which the line passes through.
   The y intercept is the point where the graph intersects the y axis, so $x = 0$ at this point.

   Plug in the values of m, etc.; we get $2 = (4 - y)/(2 - 0) \rightarrow y = 0$.

8. **e.**
   While it is tempting to solve this system of simultaneous equations to find the values of x and y, the first thing to do is to see whether the lines intersect. To do this, compare the slopes of the two lines by putting the lines into the standard form, $y = mx + b$, where m is the slope.

   By rearranging, equation 1 becomes $y = 7/4 - 3x/4$; and equation 2 becomes $y = 21/12 - 9x/12$.

   The slope of line 1 is -3/4, and the slope of line 2 is -9/12, which reduces to -3/4. Since the slopes are equal, the lines are parallel and do not intersect.

9. **b.**
   Find the slopes by rearranging the two equations into the form $y = mx + b$.

   Equation 1 becomes y = -3x/4 + 7/4 and equation 2 becomes $y = 8x/6 - 9/6$.

   So $m_1 = -3/4$ and $m_2 = 8/6 = 4/3$. We see that m_1 is the negative inverse of m_2, so line 1 is perpendicular to line 2.

Absolute Value Equations

1. **a.**
   The constant term is -15. The factors should multiply to give -15 and add to give 2.
   The numbers -3 and 5 satisfy both, $(x - 3)(x + 5)$.

2. **b.**
   The time between 3:15 PM and 4:45 PM = 1.5 hours. 1.5 * 50 = 75.

   Reminder: half an hour is written as .5 of an hour, not .3 of an hour, even though on a clock a half hour is 30 minutes.

3. **b.**
   Rearrange, reduce, and factor.

   $2x^2 + 14x + 0 = 0$.

   $2(x^2 + 7x + 0) = 0$.

   $(x + 7)(x + 0)$.

   $x = 0$, or -7.

4. **b.**
Substitute $g(x)$ for every x in $f(x)$.

$f[g((x + 4))] = 2(x + 4)^2 + 3(x + 4) = 2x^2 + 16x + 32 + 3x + 12 = 2x^2 + 19x + 44$.

5. **b.**
Two solutions: $(x + 4) = 2$ and $-(x + 4) = 2$.

Or $x + 4 = 2$, $x = -2$.

And $x + 4 = -2$, $x = -6$.

6. **b.**
Find the value of the constant by plugging in the given information.

$20 = 3 * 5 + c \rightarrow c = 5$.

Now use the value of c and the new value of s to find p. $50 = 3p + 5 \rightarrow p = 15$.

7. **e.**
$g(5) = 5 - 4 = 1$. $f[g(5)] = 2 * 1 + 3\sqrt{1} = 5$.

8. **a.**
From the domain of x, the lowest value of x is -4, and the highest value is 4. We are tempted to think that $f(x)$ will have the least value at $x = -4$: $f(-4) = 4$. However, $f(x)$ is equal to a squared value, so the lowest value of $f(x)$ is 0. This happens at $x = -2$.

Geometry

1. **a.**
The Pythagorean triple (special right triangle property) means the two shorter sides form a right triangle.

$1/2bh = $ A. So, $(1/2)(3)(4) = 6$.

2. **e.**
$AB^2 = AC^2 = AD2 + CD^2 \rightarrow AB^2 = 3^2 + 4^2 \rightarrow AB = 5$.

3. **a.**
In a right triangle, the square of the hypotenuse = the sum of the squares of the other two sides.

$AB^2 + BC^2 = AC^2 \rightarrow AC^2 = 36 + 64 \rightarrow AC = 10$.

4. **c.**
If the area of the square is 36 cm^2, then each side is 6 cm. If we look at the triangle made by half the square, that diagonal would be the hypotenuse of the triangle, and its length $= \sqrt{6^2 + 6^2} = 6\sqrt{2}$.

This hypotenuse is also the diameter of the circle, so the radius of the circle is $3\sqrt{2}$.

The area of the circle = A = πr^2 = 18π.

The area outside the square, but within the circle is 18π -36.

Fundamental Counting Principle, Permutations, Combinations

1. **c.**
The number of ways = 4 * 3 * 5 * 2 * 3 = 360.

2. **b.**
Multiply the possible number of choices for each item from which you can choose.

2 * 3 * 2 * 2 = 24.

3. **c.**
This is a combination problem. The order of the candidates does not matter.

The number of combinations = 5!/3!(5 - 3)! = 5 * 4/2 * 1 = 10.

4. **e.**
This is a permutation problem. The order in which the tiles are arranged is counted.

The number of patterns = 5!/(5 - 3)! = 5 * 4 * 3 = 60.

5. **e.**
This is a permutation problem. The order in which the chores are completed matters.

$^5P_5$ = 5!/(5 - 5)! = 5! = 5 * 4 * 3 * 2 * 1 = 120.

Ratios, Proportions, Rate of Change

1. **b.**
The ratio of boys to girls is 150:100, or 3:2.

2. **b.**
A full tank has 16 gallons → 3/4 of the tank = 12 gallons. The car can travel 30 miles on 4 gallons, so 12 gallons would take the car 12 * 30/4 = 90 miles.

3. **c.**
Average Rate of Change = the change in value/change in time = (total profit – initial profit)/change in time. Initial profit = 0; change in time = 7 years.

Increase = 5000 * 5 = 25000; decrease = 2000 * 2 = 4000; total profit = 25000 - 4000 = 21000.

(21000 - 0)/7 years = $3000/year.

4. **c.**
Total number of marbles = 250.

#red marbles = 250 * 40/100 = 250 * .4 = 100.

#blue marbles = 250 * .3 = 75.

#green marbles = 250 * .1 = 25.

#black marbles = 250 * .2 = 50.

5. **c.**

The probability of selecting a boy from the entire group = 30:80.

The probability of selecting a girl from the remaining group = 50:79.

The probability of selecting a boy and a girl is (30:80) * (50:79) = 1500:6320.

Reading Comprehension

1. a.
2. b.
3. a.
4. a.
5. d.
6. d.
7. b.
8. c.
9. c.
10. d.
11. d.
12. a.
13. a.
14. c.
15. c.
16. a.
17. c.
18. a.
19. a.
20. b.
21. b.
22. b.
23. a.
24. a.
25. c.
26. a.
27. b.
28. b.
29. b.
30. a.

31. b.
32. d.
33. a.
34. d.
35. a.
36. b.
37. d.
38. d.
39. a.
40. b.

Writing

1. a.
2. d.
3. c.
4. c.
5. d.
6. d.
7. b.
8. d.
9. d.
10. c.
11. b.
12. a.
13. a.
14. a.
15. d.
16. b.
17. c.
18. a.
19. a.
20. c.
21. b.
22. b.
23. a.
24. a.
25. b.
26. d.
27. b.
28. b.
29. c.
30. c.
31. b.
32. a.
33. c.
34. d.
35. d.

36. d.
37. c.
38. a.
39. b.
40. d.
41. **Score of 5+**

General George Patton was speaking of war when he noted that "no good decision was ever made in a swivel chair;" however, that observation applies to situations beyond battle. While a big-picture perspective is useful in analyzing situations and deciding how to act, an on-the-ground outlook is essential. In matters of politics, and technology, to name two, the best-laid plans usually have to be changed to respond to changing circumstances.

One example which illustrates the necessity of on-the-ground action is the famous space flight of Apollo 13. Before launch, all plans were worked out to get the manned mission to the moon and back. However, due to a fluke set of circumstances – an oxygen tank explosion and the resulting technical problems – the plans had to change. The successful return of Apollo 13 and the survival of its crew would not have been possible without the quick thinking of the men on board. They first noticed the incident, well before the technical crew in Houston would have detected it from Earth. While the work of the technical crew was of course key as well, without the astronauts on board the ship to implement an emergency plan, the mission would surely have been lost.

Just as there are often unforeseen circumstances when implementing technology, politics can also be unpredictable. For example, the Cuban Missile Crisis in 1962 required immediate, on-the-ground decision making by the leaders of the United States. Prior to the Cold War standoff, President Kennedy and his advisors had already decided their hardline position against Soviet weapons expansion in the Western hemisphere. The Monroe Doctrine, status quo since the 1920s, held that European countries should not practice their influence in the Americas. The Soviet Union tested this line by establishing intermediate-range missiles on the island of Cuba. President Kennedy could not simply hold to the established wisdom, because the true limits had never been tested. Instead, to stave off the threat of attack, he was forced to act immediately as events unfolded to preserve the safety of American lives. The crisis unfolded minute-by-minute, with formerly confident advisors unsure of the smartest step. Eventually, after thirteen tense days, the leaders were able to reach a peaceful conclusion.

What these events of the 1960s illustrate is that the best laid plans are often rendered useless by an unfolding situation. For crises to be resolved, whether they be in war, technology, or politics; leaders must have level heads in the moment with up-to-date information. Therefore, plans established in advance by those in swivel chairs with level heads are not always the best plans to follow. History has shown us that we must be able to think on our feet as unforeseen situations unfold.

Score of 3-4:

It is often necessary to be directly on the ground as a situation unfolds to know what is best do to. This is because situations can be unpredictable and what you previously thought was the best course of action, is not always so. This can be seen in the unfolding events of the 1962 Cuban Missile Crisis.

The Cuban Missile Crisis happened in 1962, during the presidency of John F. Kennedy, when Nikita Khrushchev, president of the Soviet Union, developed an intermediate-range missile base on the island of Cuba, within range of the United States. Since the Monroe Doctrine in the 1920s, the United States leaders have declared that they would not tolerate this kind of aggression. However, the decisions that had been made by leaders in the past, removed from the situation, were no longer relevant. It was necessary for President Kennedy to make decisions as events unfolded.

As the Cuban Missile Crisis shows us, at turning points in history decisions have to be made as events unfold by those who are in the middle of a situation. Otherwise, we would all be acting according to what those in the past and those removed from the challenge thought was best. Following the Monroe Doctrine could have resulted in unnecessary violence.

Score of 2 or Less:

It is necessary to make decisions while in the middle of a situation, not above the situation, because there is always information that is only known to people in the middle of the situation. For example, in a war, the strategists in Washington might have an overall aim in the war, but they would be unable to know what it best to do on the ground. Situations like running out of ammunition or the enemy having an unexpected backup could change the decisions that need to be made. This was especially true before cell phones and other digital technologies made communication easier.

Practice Test 2

Mathematics

Section 1:
Percent/Part/Whole; Percent Change

Section 2:
Mean, Median, Mode

Section 3:
Exponents and Roots

Section 4:
Algebraic Equations

Section 5:
Inequalities, Literal Equations, Polynomials, Binomials

Section 6:
Slope and Distance to Midpoint

Section 7:
Absolute Value Equations

Section 8:
Geometry

Section 9:
Fundamental Counting Principle, Permutations, Combinations

Section 10:
Ratios, Proportions, Rate of Change

Percent/Part/Whole, Percent

1. If the value of a car depreciates by 60% over ten years, and its value in the year 2000 is $2500, what was its value in the year 1990?
   a. $6000.
   b. $6230.
   c. $6250.
   d. $6500.
   e. $6600.

2. If an account is opened with a starting balance of $500, what is the amount in the account after 3 years if the account pays compound interest of 5%?
    a. $560.80.
    b. $578.81.
    c. $564.50.
    d. $655.10.
    e. $660.00.

3. A piece of memorabilia depreciates by 1% every year. If the value of the memorabilia is $75000, what will it be 2 years from now? Give the answer as a whole number.
    a. $74149.
    b. $74150.
    c. $73151.
    d. $71662.
    e. $73507.

4. A dress is marked down by 20% in an effort to boost sales for one week. After that week, the price of the dress is brought back to the original value. What percent did the price of the dress have to be increased from its discounted price?
    a. 20%.
    b. 25%.
    c. 120%.
    d. 125%.
    e. 15%.

5. A car dealer increases the price of a car by 30%, but then discounts it by 30%. What is the relationship between the final price and the original price?
    a. $.91x : x$.
    b. $.98x : x$.
    c. 1:1.
    d. $.88x : x$.
    e. $.75x : x$.

Mean, Median, Mode

1. Twelve teams competed in a mathematics test. The scores recorded for each team are: 29, 30, 28, 27, 35, 43, 45, 50, 46, 37, 44, and 41. What is the median score?
    a. 37.
    b. 41.
    c. 39.
    d. 44.
    e. 45.

2. A class of 10 students scores 90, 78, 45, 98, 84, 79, 66, 87, 78, and 94. What is the mean score? What is the median score? What is the mode?
    a. 69.9, 81.5, 78.
    b. 79.9, 80, 78.
    c. 79.9, 87, 76.
    d. Not enough information given.
    e. None of the above.

3. A shop sells 3 kinds of t-shirts: one design sells for $4.50, the second for $13.25, and the third for $15.50. If the shop sold 8 shirts of the first design, 12 shirts of the second design, and 4 shirts of the third design, what was the average selling price of the shirts?
    a. $10.71.
    b. $10.25.
    c. $14.55.
    d. $12.55.
    e. $5.80.

Exponents and Roots

1. Evaluate $(a^2 * a^{54} + a^{56} + (a^{58}/a^2))/a^4$.
    a. a^{56}.
    b. $3a^{56}$.
    c. $3a^{52}$.
    d. $3a^{54}$.
    e. a^{54}.

2. $9^m = 3^{-1/n}$. What is mn?
    a. .5.
    b. 2.
    c. -2.
    d. -.5.
    e. -1.

3. If $2^a*4^a = 32$, what is a?
    a. 1/3.
    b. 2/3.
    c. 1.
    d. 4/3.
    e. 5/3.

Algebraic Equations

1. Expand $(3x - 4)(6 - 2x)$.
    a. $6x^2 - 6x + 8$.
    b. $-6x^2 + 26x - 24$.
    c. $6x^2 - 26x + 24$.
    d. $-6x^2 + 26x + 24$.
    e. $6x^2 + 26x - 24$.

2. If $6n + m$ is divisible by 3 and 5, which of the following numbers when added to $6n + m$ will still give a result that is divisible by 3 and 5?
   a. 4.
   b. 6.
   c. 12.
   d. 20.
   e. 60.

3. If x is negative, and $x^3/5$ and $x/5$ both give the same result, what could be the value of x?
   a. -5.
   b. -4.
   c. 3.
   d. 0.
   e. -1.

4. If $m = 3548$, and $n = 235$, then what is the value of $m * n$?
   a. 87940.
   b. 843499.
   c. 87900.
   d. 8830.
   e. 833780.

5. A ball is thrown at a speed of 30 mph. How far will it travel in 2 minutes and 35 seconds?
   a. 1.5 miles.
   b. 1.20 miles.
   c. 1.29 miles.
   d. 1.3 miles.
   e. 1.1 miles.

6. Simplify: $30(\sqrt{40} - \sqrt{60})$.
   a. $30(\sqrt{5} - \sqrt{15})$.
   b. $30(\sqrt{10} + \sqrt{15})$.
   c. $60(\sqrt{5} + \sqrt{15})$.
   d. $60(\sqrt{10} - \sqrt{15})$.
   e. 60.

7. Simplify: $30/(\sqrt{40} - \sqrt{60})$.
   a. $3(\sqrt{5} + \sqrt{15})$.
   b. $-3(\sqrt{5} - \sqrt{15})$.
   c. $-3(\sqrt{10} + \sqrt{15})$.
   d. $3(\sqrt{10} + \sqrt{15})$.
   e. $3(\sqrt{10} - \sqrt{15})$.

8. What is the least common multiple of 2, 3, 4, and 5?
   a. 30.
   b. 60.
   c. 120.
   d. 40.
   e. 50.

9. It costs $6 to make a pen that sells for $12. How many pens need to be sold to make a profit of $60?
   a. 10.
   b. 6.
   c. 72.
   d. 30.
   e. 12.

Inequalities, Literal Equations, Polynomials, and Binomials

1. If $a = b + 3$, and $3b = 5a + 6$, what is $3a - 2b$?
   a. -1.5.
   b. 2.5.
   c. 3.
   d. 4.3.
   e. 5.

2. The sum of the roots of a quadratic equation is 8, and the difference is 2. What is the equation?
   a. $x^2 - 8x - 15$.
   b. $x^2 + 8x + 15$.
   c. $x^2 - 8x + 15$.
   d. $x^2 + 8x - 15$.
   e. $x^2 + 15$.

3. Solve the following system of equations: $3x + 2y = 7$ and $3x + y = 5$.
   a. $x = 2, y = 1$.
   b. $x = 2, y = 2$.
   c. $x = 1, y = 0$.
   d. $x = 1, y = 2$.
   e. $x = 1, y = 1$.

4. Nine tickets were sold for $41. If the tickets cost $4 and $5, how many $5 tickets were sold?
   a. 5.
   b. 4.
   c. 9.
   d. 6.
   e. 7.

5. Joe brought a bag of 140 M&Ms to his class of 40 students. Each boy received 2 M&Ms. Each girl received 4. How many boys were in the class?

    a. 10.
    b. 20.
    c. 30.
    d. 40.
    e. 50.

Slope and Distance to Midpoint

1. Is the graph of the function $f(x) = -3x^2 + 4$ linear, asymptotical, symmetrical to the x axis, symmetrical to the y axis, or not symmetrical to either axis?

    a. Symmetrical to the x axis.
    b. Symmetrical to the y axis.
    c. Symmetrical to neither axis.
    d. Asymptotic.
    e. Linear.

2. Two points on a line have coordinates (3, 12) and (9, 20). What is the distance between these two points?

    a. 10.
    b. 12.
    c. 13.
    d. 8.
    e. 11.

3. In the following graph, what is the equation of line AB if line AB is perpendicular to line PQ? Point coordinates are:

    M (-4, 0); O (0, 2); and N (0, -3). The lines intersect at (-2,1).

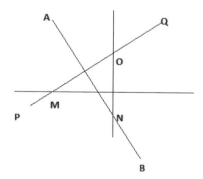

    a. $y = 2x + 3$.
    b. $y = -2x - 3$.
    c. $y = x - 4$.
    d. $y = x + 3$.
    e. $y = -2x - 3$.

4. What is the equation of a line passing through $(1, 2)$ and $(6, 12)$?
   a. $y = x$.
   b. $y = 2x$.
   c. $y = x/2$.
   d. $y = 2x + 2$.
   e. $y = x - 2$.

5. What is the midpoint of the line connecting points $(0, 8)$ and $(2, 6)$?
   a. $(-1, 1)$.
   b. $(2, 14)$.
   c. $(-2, 2)$.
   d. $(0, 1)$.
   e. $(1, 7)$.

6. What is the equation of a line passing through $(1, 1)$ and $(2, 4)$?
   a. $3y = x + 2$.
   b. $2y = x + 3$.
   c. $y = 3x - 2$.
   d. $4x = y + 2$.
   e. $y = (1/3)x + 2$.

7. Line A passes through $(0, 0)$ and $(3, 4)$. Line B passes through $(2, 6)$ and $(3, y)$. What value of y will make the lines parallel?
   a. $20/3$.
   b. 7.
   c. $22/3$.
   d. 29.
   e. 5.

8. Line A passes through $(1, 3)$ and $(3, 4)$. Line B passes through $(3, 7)$ and $(5, y)$. What value of y will make the lines perpendicular?
   a. 1.
   b. 2.
   c. 3.
   d. 4.
   e. 5.

9. What is the equation of line A that is perpendicular to line B, connecting $(8, 1)$ and $(10, 5)$, that intersects at $(x, 14)$?
   a. $y = 2x - 7$.
   b. $y = -2x + 7$.
   c. $y = (-1/2)x + 19\frac{1}{4}$.
   d. $y = 5x - 7$.
   e. $y = 2x - 19\frac{1}{4}$.

1. If $f(x) = (x + 2)^2$, and $0 \leq x \leq 4$, what is the minimum value of $f(x)$?
    a. 1.
    b. 2.
    c. 3.
    d. 4.
    e. 5.

2. What is $x^2 - 9$ divided by $x - 3$?
    a. $x - 3$.
    b. $x + 3$.
    c. x.
    d. $x - 1$.
    e. 6.

3. An equation has two roots: 5 and -8. What is a possible equation?
    a. $x^2 - 3x + 40$.
    b. $x^2 - 3x - 40$.
    c. $x^2 + x + 40$.
    d. $x^2 + 3x - 40$.
    e. $2x^2 - 3x + 40$.

4. In an ant farm, the number of ants grows every week according to the formula $N = 100 + 2^w$, where w is the number of weeks elapsed. How many ants will the colony have after 5 weeks?
    a. 115.
    b. 125.
    c. 135.
    d. 132.
    e. 233.

5. Find the values of x that validate the following equation: $[(4x + 5)^2 - (40x + 25)]^{1/2} + 3|x| - 14 = 0$.
    a. -2, -14.
    b. 2, -14.
    c. -2, 14.
    d. 2, 14.
    e. No solution.

6. If $|x| = 4$ and $|y| = 5$, what are the values of $|x + y|$?
    a. 1, 9.
    b. -1, 9.
    c. -1, -9.
    d. -1, -9.
    e. $1 < |x + y| < 9$.

7. If $y = |x|$, what is the range of y?
    a. $y < 0$.
    b. $0 < y < x$.
    c. $y > 0$.
    d. $y \geq 0$.
    e. $y > x$.

Geometry

1. The length of a rectangle is 4 times its width. If the width of the rectangle is $5 - x$ inches, and the perimeter of the rectangle is 30 inches, what is x?
    a. 1.
    b. 2.
    c. 3.
    d. 4.
    e. 5.

2. Two sides of a triangle have a ratio AC:BC = 5:4. The length of AB on a similar triangle = 24. What is the actual value of AC for the larger triangle?
    a. 10.
    b. 14.4.
    c. 35.
    d. 40.
    c. 50.

3. If the diameter of a circle is doubled, the area increases by what factor?
    a. 1 time.
    b. 2 times.
    c. 3 times.
    d. 4 times.
    e. 5 times.

4. In the following triangle PQR, what is the measure of angle A?
    a. 145⁰.
    b. 140⁰.
    c. 70⁰.
    d. 50⁰.
    e. 40⁰.

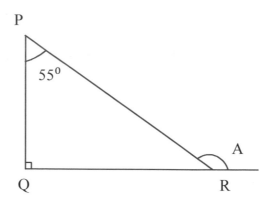

Fundamental Counting Principle, Permutations, Combinations

1. Next weekend, I have more chores to do around the house. There are 5 chores I must complete by the end of the day. I can choose to do any 2 of them in any order, and then do any 2 the next day again in any order, and then do the remaining 1 the following day. How many choices do I have?
    a. 20.
    b. 6.
    c. 120.
    d. 130.
    e. 25.

2. A certain lottery play sheet has 10 numbers from which 5 have to be chosen. How many different ways can I pick the numbers?
    a. 150.
    b. 250.
    c. 252.
    d. 143.
    e. 278.

3. At a buffet, there are 3 choices for an appetizer, 6 choices for a beverage, and 3 choices for an entrée. How many different ways can I select food from all the food choices?
    a. 12.
    b. 27.
    c. 36.
    d. 42.
    e. 54.

4. If there is a basket of 10 assorted fruits, and I want to pick out 3 fruits, how many combinations of fruits do I have to choose from?
    a. 130.
    b. 210.
    c. 310.
    d. 120.
    e. 100.

5. How many ways can I pick 3 numbers from a set of 10 numbers?
    a. 720.
    b. 120.
    c. 180.
    d. 150.
    e. 880.

Ratios, Proportions, Rate of Change

1. If number n, divided by number m, gives a result of .5, what is the relationship between n and m?
    a. n is twice as big as m.
    b. m is three times as big as n.
    c. n is a negative number.
    d. m is a negative number.
    e. n is ½ of m.

2. In a fruit basket, there are 10 apples, 5 oranges, 5 pears, and 6 figs. If I select two fruits, what is the probability that I will first pick a pear and then an apple?
    a. .07.
    b. .08.
    c. 1/13.
    d. 13.
    e. 5.

3. In a fruit basket, there are 3 apples, 5 oranges, 2 pears, and 2 figs. If I pick out two fruits, what is the probability that I will pick a fig first and then an apple?
    Round to the nearest 100th.
    a. .04.
    b. .05.
    c. .06.
    d. .03.
    e. .02.

4. If x workers can make p toys in c days, how many toys can y workers make in d days if they work at the same rate?
    a. cp/qx.
    b. cq/px.
    c. cqy/px.
    d. pdy/cx.
    e. qy/px.

5. If a car travels 35 miles on a gallon of gas, how far will it travel on 13 gallons of gas?
    a. 189 miles.
    b. 255 miles.
    c. 335 miles.
    d. 455 miles.
    e. 500 miles.

Reading Comprehension

We are told nothing as to sacrificial and religious rites, and all else is omitted which does not provide material for artistic treatment. The so-called Northern Mythology, therefore, may be regarded as a precious relic of the beginning of Northern poetry, rather than as a representation of the religious beliefs of the Scandinavians, and these literary fragments bear many signs of the transitional stage wherein the confusion of the old and new faiths is easily apparent.

But notwithstanding the limitations imposed by long neglect it is possible to reconstruct in part a plan of the ancient Norse beliefs, and the general reader will derive much profit from Carlyle's illuminating study in "Heroes and Hero-worship." "A bewildering, inextricable jungle of delusions, confusions, falsehoods and absurdities, covering the whole field of Life!" he calls them, with all good reason. But he goes on to show, with equal truth, that at the soul of this crude worship of distorted nature was a spiritual force seeking expression. What we probe without reverence they viewed with awe, and not understanding it, straightway deified it, as all children have been apt to do in all stages of the world's history. Truly they were hero-worshippers after Carlyle's own heart, and skepticism had no place in their simple philosophy.

1. What is the main idea of the passage?
    a. We have a lot of evidence about Norse religion.
    b. Norse literature provides information on Norse beliefs.
    c. Norse beliefs can be loosely reconstructed.
    d. The Norse practiced religious sacrifice.

2. Which statement is not a detail from the passage?
    a. Carlyle wrote about Norse beliefs.
    b. Scandinavian religion worshipped nature.
    c. Scandinavian literature reflects the transition from old to new religion.
    d. Nordic poetry is religious.

3. What is the meaning of skepticism near the end of the paragraph?
    a. Doubt
    b. Justification
    c. Faith
    d. Thought

4. What is the author's primary purpose in writing this passage?
    a. To introduce Norse religion
    b. To analyze Norse poetry
    c. To explain Norse history
    d. To introduce Norse culture

5. Which is the best summary of this passage?
    a. From what we know, the Norse religion was based around nature.
    b. The Norse worshipped heroes.
    c. Norse epics are about heroes.
    d. The Norse were successful conquerors.

Professor Murray will, I am sure, excuse me if I say that he has the common fault of most Englishmen of being inaudible. Why on earth people who have something to say which is worth hearing should not take the slight trouble to learn how to make it heard is one of the strange mysteries of modern life. Their methods are as reasonable as to try to pour some precious stuff from the spring to the reservoir through a non-conducting pipe, which could by the least effort be opened. Professor Murray made several profound remarks to his white tie and to the water-carafe upon the table, with a humorous, twinkling aside to the silver candlestick upon his right. Then he sat down, and Mr. Waldron, the famous popular lecturer, rose amid a general murmur of applause. He was a stern, gaunt man, with a harsh voice, and an aggressive manner, but he had the merit of knowing how to assimilate the ideas of other men, and to pass them on in a way which was intelligible and even interesting to the lay public, with a happy knack of being funny about the most unlikely objects, so that the precession of the Equinox or the formation of a vertebrate became a highly humorous process as treated by him.

6. What is the main idea of the passage?
    a. Public speaking is a useful skill.
    b. Mr. Waldron was a very good lecturer.
    c. Professor Murray talked to the water carafe.
    d. Lectures can be entertaining.

7. Which statement is not a detail from the passage?
    a. Mr. Waldron is a lecturer.
    b. Professor Murray cannot be heard.
    c. There is a silver candlestick.
    d. Mr. Waldron is quite jolly.

8. What is the meaning of assimilate near the end of the paragraph?
    a. Take in
    b. Dispute
    c. Agree with
    d. Overrule

9. What is the author's primary purpose in writing this passage?
    a. To educate
    b. To inform
    c. To entertain
    d. To argue

10. Which is the best summary of this passage?
    a. Mr. Waldron's lecture was more appealing than Professor Murray.
    b. Professor Murray could not be heard.
    c. Mr. Waldron was funny.
    d. Professor Murray looked down at the table.

"What are you doing there?" asked the Princess.

"I am spinning, my pretty child," answered the old woman, who did not know who she was.

"Oh, how pretty it is!" exclaimed the Princess. "How do you do it? Give it to me, that I may see if I can do it as well."

She had no sooner taken hold of the spindle, than, being very hasty, and rather thoughtless, and moreover, the fairies having ordained that it should be so, she pierced her hand with the point of it, and fainted away. The poor old woman was in great distress, and called for help. People came running from all quarters; they threw water in the Princess's face, they unlaced her dress, they slapped her hands, they rubbed her temples with Queen of Hungary's water, but nothing would bring her to. The King, who had run upstairs at the noise, then remembered the prediction of the fairies, and wisely concluded that this accident must have happened as the fairies had said it would. He ordered the Princess to be carried into a beautiful room of the palace, and laid on a bed embroidered with silver and gold. One might have thought it was an angel lying there, so lovely did she look, for the rich colors of her complexion had not faded in her swoon; her cheeks were still rosy, and her lips like coral. Only, her eyes were closed, but they could hear her breathing softly, which showed that she was not dead.

The King gave orders that she was to be left to sleep there in quiet, until the hour of her awaking should arrive. The good fairy who had saved her life, by condemning her to sleep for a hundred years, was in the Kingdom of Mataquin, twelve thousand leagues away, when the Princess met with her accident, but she was informed of it instantly by a little dwarf, who had a pair of seven-league boots, that is, boots which enabled the wearer to take seven leagues at a stride.

11. What is the main idea of the passage?
    a. The dwarf could take seven leagues at a stride.
    b. The fairies had condemned her to sleep.
    c. The princess pricked her finger and was cursed.
    d. The princess did not die.

12. Which statement is not a detail from the passage?
    a. A fairy saved the princess' life.
    b. The princess was cursed by Maleficient.
    c. The princess touched a spindle.
    d. A dwarf told the fairy what had happened.

13. What is the meaning of ordained in the second paragraph?
    a. Ordered
    b. Planned
    c. Allowed
    d. Disallowed

14. What is the author's primary purpose in writing this passage?
    a. To share a historical incident
    b. To entertain
    c. To educate
    d. To warn people about the danger of spindles

15. Which is the best summary of this passage?
    a. The princess was cursed and would sleep for 100 years.
    b. The prince needed to save the princess.
    c. Fairies are evil.
    d. The king was unkind and a poor ruler.

I could not perhaps appeal to an audience more capable of appreciating the truth of these remarks than to the members of an Institution, the object of which is to examine into the improvements and so-called inventions which are from time to time effected in the machinery and implements of war.

How often does any proposal or improvement come before this Institution which after investigating its antecedents is found to possess originality of design? Is it not a fact that even the most ingenious and successful inventions turn out on inquiry to be mere adaptations of contrivances already existing, or that they are produced by applying to one branch of industry the principles or the contrivances which have been evolved in another. I think that no one can have constantly attended the lectures of this or any similar Institution, without becoming impressed, above all things, with the want of originality observable amongst men, and with the great calls which, even in this age of cultivated intellects and abundant materials to work upon, all inventors are obliged to make upon those who have preceded them.

16. What is the main idea of the passage?
    a. There is little that is truly original.
    b. War has not changed.
    c. Implements of war require new materials.
    d. Ingenious inventions are entirely new.

17. Which statement is not a detail from the passage?
    a. The institution examines war implements.
    b. Inventions in one industry can be used in another.
    c. Inventors create entirely new items.
    d. Inventions build upon what came before.

18. What is the meaning of antecedents in the second paragraph?
    a. What came after
    b. What came before
    c. Other's ideas
    d. Plagiarism

19. What is the author's primary purpose in writing this passage?
    a. To introduce his topic
    b. To educate the audience
    c. To persuade the audience
    d. To show why his invention is better

20. Which is the best summary of this passage?
    a. Inventions and innovations build upon what came before them.
    b. New inventions are essential to industry.
    c. War supports innovation.
    d. Innovation stops during times of war.

The situation of the house was good. High hills rose immediately behind, and at no great distance on each side; some of which were open downs, the others cultivated and woody. The village of Barton was chiefly on one of these hills, and formed a pleasant view from the cottage windows. The prospect in front was more extensive; it commanded the whole of the valley, and reached into the country beyond. The hills which surrounded the cottage terminated the valley in that direction; under another name, and in another course, it branched out again between two of the steepest of them.

With the size and furniture of the house Mrs. Dashwood was upon the whole well satisfied; for though her former style of life rendered many additions to the latter indispensable, yet to add and improve was a delight to her; and she had at this time ready money enough to supply all that was wanted of greater elegance to the apartments. "As for the house itself, to be sure," said she, "it is too small for our family, but we will make ourselves tolerably comfortable for the present, as it is too late in the year for improvements. Perhaps in the spring, if I have plenty of money, as I dare say I shall, we may think about building. These parlors are both too small for such parties of our friends as I hope to see often collected here; and I have some thoughts of throwing the passage into one of them with perhaps a part of the other, and so leave the remainder of that other for an entrance; this, with a new drawing room which may be easily added, and a bed-chamber and garret above, will make it a very snug little cottage. I could wish the stairs were handsome. But one must not expect everything; though, I suppose it would be no difficult matter to widen them. I shall see how much I am before-hand with the world in the spring, and we will plan our improvements accordingly."

21. What is the main idea of the passage?
    a. The house is well-placed.
    b. The house is too small.
    c. The house could be improved.
    d. The house is quite poor.

22. Which statement is not a detail from the passage?
    a. The parlors are too small.
    b. There is a garret above the drawing room.
    c. The cottage has hills behind it.
    d. Mrs. Dashwood has nice furnishings.

23. What is the meaning of <u>indispensable</u> in the second paragraph?
    a. Necessary
    b. Unnecessary
    c. Unappealing
    d. Appealing

24. What is the author's primary purpose in writing this passage?
    a. To create a visual impression of the house
    b. To provide insights into Mrs. Dashwood's character
    c. To show how Mrs. Dashwood felt about the cottage
    d. To illustrate Mrs. Dashwood's financial state

25. Which is the best summary of this passage?
    a. Mrs. Dashwood finds the cottage lovely, but inadequate.
    b. Mrs. Dashwood would like a smaller home.
    c. Mrs. Dashwood is quite wealthy.
    d. Mrs. Dashwood is impoverished.

The division of the world being now satisfactorily arranged, it would seem that all things ought to have gone on smoothly, but such was not the case. Trouble arose in an unlooked-for quarter. The Giants, those hideous monsters (some with legs formed of serpents) who had sprung from the earth and the blood of Uranus, declared war against the triumphant deities of Olympus, and a struggle ensued, which, in consequence of Gæa having made these children of hers invincible as long as they kept their feet on the ground, was wearisome and protracted. Their mother's precaution, however, was rendered unavailing by pieces of rock being hurled upon them, which threw them down, and their feet being no longer placed firmly on their mother-earth, they were overcome, and this tedious war (which was called the Gigantomachia) at last came to an end. Among the most daring of these earth-born giants were Enceladus, Rhœtus, and the valiant Mimas, who, with youthful fire and energy, hurled against heaven great masses of rock and burning oak-trees, and defied the lightning of Zeus. One of the most powerful monsters who opposed Zeus in this war was called Typhon or Typhœus. He was the youngest son of Tartarus and Gæa, and had a hundred heads, with eyes which struck terror to the beholders, and awe-inspiring voices frightful to hear. This dreadful monster resolved to conquer both gods and men, but his plans were at length defeated by Zeus, who, after a violent encounter, succeeded in destroying him with a thunderbolt, but not before he had so terrified the gods that they had fled for refuge to Egypt, where they metamorphosed themselves into different animals and thus escaped.

26. What is the main idea of the passage?
    a. Zeus had to fight the Giants
    b. Gaea was the mother of the gods.
    c. Gaea was the mother of the Giants.
    d. The Giants won the battle.

27. Which statement is not a detail from the passage?
    a. Zeus was called Typhon
    b. Zeus was the son of Gaea
    c. Zeus was the husband of Hera
    d. Zeus was the son of Tartarus

28. What is the meaning of <u>triumphant</u> in the paragraph?
    a. Failing
    b. Greek
    c. Victorious
    d. Immoral

29. What is the author's primary purpose in writing this passage?
    a. To entertain the reader
    b. To share stories from mythology
    c. To provide religious education
    d. To show why Greek mythology is wrong

30. Which is the best summary of this passage?
    a. The Giants were monstrous and evil.
    b. The Greek gods of Olympus had to defeat the Giants.
    c. The Giants are the precursors of the gods.
    d. Greek mythology is violent.

"Oh, I can carry it," the child responded cheerfully. "It isn't heavy. I've got all my worldly goods in it, but it isn't heavy. And if it isn't carried in just a certain way the handle pulls out—so I'd better keep it because I know the exact knack of it. It's an extremely old carpet-bag. Oh, I'm very glad you've come, even if it would have been nice to sleep in a wild cherry-tree. We've got to drive a long piece, haven't we? Mrs. Spencer said it was eight miles. I'm glad because I love driving. Oh, it seems so wonderful that I'm going to live with you and belong to you. I've never belonged to anybody—not really. But the asylum was the worst. I've only been in it four months, but that was enough. I don't suppose you ever were an orphan in an asylum, so you can't possibly understand what it is like. It's worse than anything you could imagine. Mrs. Spencer said it was wicked of me to talk like that, but I didn't mean to be wicked. It's so easy to be wicked without knowing it, isn't it? They were good, you know—the asylum people. But there is so little scope for the imagination in an asylum—only just in the other orphans. It was pretty interesting to imagine things about them—to imagine that perhaps the girl who sat next to you was really the daughter of a belted earl, who had been stolen away from her parents in her infancy by a cruel nurse who died before she could confess. I used to lie awake at nights and imagine things like that, because I didn't have time in the day. I guess that's why I'm so thin—I AM dreadful thin, ain't I? There isn't a pick on my bones. I do love to imagine I'm nice and plump, with dimples in my elbows."

31. What is the main idea of the passage?
    a. The girl is an orphan.
    b. The girl has been in an orphanage.
    c. The girl is excited and imaginative.
    d. The girl in the orphanage is the daughter of an earl.

32. Which statement is not a detail from the passage?
    a. The child has an old carpet-bag.
    b. The child loves driving.
    c. The child is thin.
    d. The asylum was a horrible place.

33. What is the meaning of <u>asylum</u> in the paragraph?
    a. Hospital
    b. Sanitarium
    c. Orphanage
    d. Prison

34. What is the author's primary purpose in writing this passage?
    a. To illustrate the child's excitement.
    b. To educate the reader.
    c. To explain why orphanages were bad.
    d. To create the setting.

35. Which is the best summary of this passage?
    a. The child is frightened of the changes in her life.
    b. The child is excited by the changes in her life.
    c. The family is unhappy about the child.
    d. The family is happy about the child.

For my own part, I had been feverishly excited all day. Something very like the war fever that occasionally runs through a civilized community had got into my blood, and in my heart I was not so very sorry that I had to return to Maybury that night. I was even afraid that that last fusillade I had heard might mean the extermination of our invaders from Mars. I can best express my state of mind by saying that I wanted to be in at the death.

It was nearly eleven when I started to return. The night was unexpectedly dark; to me, walking out of the lighted passage of my cousins' house, it seemed indeed black, and it was as hot and close as the day. Overhead the clouds were driving fast, albeit not a breath stirred the shrubs about us. My cousins' man lit both lamps. Happily, I knew the road intimately. My wife stood in the light of the doorway, and watched me until I jumped up into the dog cart. Then abruptly she turned and went in, leaving my cousins side by side wishing me good hap.

I was a little depressed at first with the contagion of my wife's fears, but very soon my thoughts reverted to the Martians. At that time I was absolutely in the dark as to the course of the evening's fighting. I did not know even the circumstances that had precipitated the conflict. As I came through Ockham (for that was the way I returned, and not through Send and Old Woking) I saw along the western horizon a blood-red glow, which as I drew nearer, crept slowly up the sky. The driving clouds of the gathering thunderstorm mingled there with masses of black and red smoke.

36. What is the main idea of the passage?
    a. Martians are going to invade.
    b. The man is fighting the Martians.
    c. The Martians caused a thunderstorm.
    d. The narrator is traveling at a time when Martians had invaded.

37. Which statement is not a detail from the passage?
    a. He is leaving his cousins' home.
    b. Humans had fought the Martians all evening.
    c. He travelled through Send.
    d. He travelled through Ockham.

38. What is the meaning of <u>fusillade</u> in the first paragraph?
    a. Battle
    b. Series of shots
    c. Trains
    d. Spaceship

39. What is the author's primary purpose in writing this passage?
    a. To educate
    b. To tell a story
    c. To create a character
    d. To create the setting

40. Which is the best summary of this passage?
    a. The narrator is fighting the Martians.
    b. Martians have destroyed Ockham.
    c. The narrator wants to fight the Martians.
    d. The Martians have won the battle for earth.

Writing

Questions 1 – 8 are based on the following passage. Sentences are numbered at the end for easy reference within the questions.

The world is very different now (1). For man holds in his mortal hands the power to <u>abolish</u> all forms of human poverty and all forms of human life (2). And yet the same revolutionary beliefs for which our <u>forebears</u> fought are still at issue around the globe, the belief that the rights of man come not from the generosity of the state, but from the hand of God (3).

We dare not forget today that we are the heirs of that first revolution (4). Let the word go forth from this time and place, to friend and foe alike, that the torch has been passed to a new generation of <u>Americans-- born</u> in this century, tempered by war, disciplined by a hard and bitter peace, proud of our ancient heritage, and unwilling to witness or permit the slow undoing of those human rights to which this nation has always been committed, and to which we are committed today at home and around the world (5).

Let every nation know whether it wishes us well or ill that we shall pay any price, bear any burden, meet any hardship, support any friend, and oppose any foe, to assure the survival and the success of liberty (6).

1. Which of the following best concludes the first paragraph?
    a. The world is safer today.
    b. The world is more dangerous today.
    c. Rights come from God.
    d. Rights come from government.

2. Which of the following is the best version of sentence 1?
   a. The world is very different now.
   b. Today's challenges are the same as before.
   c. The world is more similar to before than ever.
   d. None of the above

3. Which edit should be made in sentence 3?
   a. globe; the
   b. globe—the
   c. globe the
   d. None of the above

4. Which word is a synonym for the underlined word in sentence 2?
   a. Duplicate
   b. Diminish
   c. Eliminate
   d. None of the above

5. Which revision would most improve sentence 6?
   a. Insert commas before and after *whether it wishes us well or ill*
   b. Remove *and* before *oppose any foe*
   c. Change *assure* to *ensure*
   d. None of the above

6. Which is the best replacement for the underlined word in sentence 3?
   a. Relatives
   b. Ancestors
   c. Forefathers
   d. None of the above

7. The writer is considering deleting the last sentence. If the writer decided to delete this sentence, the passage would primarily lose a statement that:
   a. Enhances the subject and setting
   b. Provides support for a point previously made
   c. Humorously digresses from the main topic of the paragraph
   d. Reinforces the resolve of the country

8. Which of the following is the best way to punctuate the underlined portion in sentence 5?
   a. Americans--born
   b. Americans; born
   c. Americans. Born
   d. None of the above

Questions 9-16 are based on the short passage below:

This is true, that the wisdom of all these latter times, in princes' affairs, is rather fine deliveries, and shiftings of dangers and mischiefs, when they are near, than solid and grounded courses to keep them aloof (1). But this is but to try masteries with fortune (2). And let men beware, how they neglect and suffer matter of trouble to be prepared; for no man can <u>forbid</u> the spark, nor tell whence it may come (3). The difficulties in princes' business are many and great; but the greatest difficulty, is often in their own mind (4). For it is common with princes (saith Tacitus) to will contradictories, *Sunt plerumque regum voluntates vehementes, et inter se contrariae* (5). For it is the solecism of power, to think to command the end, and yet not to endure the mean (6).

Kings have to deal with their neighbors, their wives, their children, their prelates or clergy, their nobles, their second-nobles or gentlemen, their merchants, their commons, and their men of <u>war and</u> from all these arise dangers if care and circumspection be not used (7).

9. Which of the following is the best version of the underlined portion in sentence 1?
    a. It is true that
    b. This is true, that
    c. Although true that
    d. Any of the above

10. Which best describes the function of sentence 2?
    a. It isn't necessary to understand the passage.
    b. It develops the statement from sentence 1.
    c. Both A and B
    d. Neither A nor B

11. Which edit should be made in sentence 3?
    a. spark; nor
    b. spark nor
    c. spark. Nor
    d. None of the above

12. Which word is not a synonym for the underlined word in sentence 3?
    a. discourage
    b. prohibit
    c. ban
    d. outlaw

13. Which revision would most improve sentence 4?
    a. Change the semicolon after *great* to a comma
    b. Remove the apostrophe after *princes*
    c. Remove the comma after *difficulty*
    d. Both A and C

14. Which of the following best summarizes sentence 6?
    a. Power makes you desire an outcome, but not consider the journey toward it.
    b. Power makes you think only of the outcome.
    c. Power makes you think only of the journey.
    d. None of the above

15. The writer is considering deleting the last sentence. If the writer decided to delete this sentence, the passage would primarily lose a statement that:
    a. Discusses the setting
    b. Contradicts a point previously made
    c. Provides a transition for a subsequent passage
    d. Summarizes the passage

16. Which is the best way to punctuate the underlined portion in sentence 7?
    a. war. And
    b. war, and
    c. war; and
    d. Any of the above

Questions 17-24 are based on the short passage below:

<u>What I felt the next day was, I suppose, nothing that could be fairly called a reaction from the cheer of my arrival</u>; it was probably at the most only a slight oppression produced by a fuller measure of the scale, as I walked round them, gazed up at them, took them in, of my new circumstances (1). <u>They had as it were an extent</u> and mass for which I had not been prepared and in the presence of which I found myself, freshly, a little scared as well as a little proud (2). Lessons, in this agitation, certainly suffered some delay; I reflected that my first duty was, by the gentlest arts I could <u>contrive</u>, to win the child into the sense of knowing me (3). I spent the day with her out-of-doors; I arranged with her, to her great satisfaction, that it should be she, she only, who might show me the place (4). She showed it step by step and room by room and secret by secret, with <u>droll</u>, delightful, childish talk about it and with the result, in half an hour, of our becoming immense friends (5). Young as she was, I was struck, throughout our little tour, with her confidence and courage with the way, in empty chambers and dull corridors, on crooked staircases that made me pause and even on the summit of an old <u>machicolated</u> square tower that made me dizzy, her morning music, her disposition to tell me so many more things than she asked, rang out and led me on (6).

17. Which of the following is the best version of the underlined portion in sentence 1?
    a. What I felt the next day was, I suppose, nothing that could be fairly called a reaction from the cheer of my arrival
    b. I suppose what I felt the next day was nothing that could be fairly called a reaction from the cheer of my arrival
    c. What I felt the next day, I suppose, was nothing that could be fairly called a reaction from the cheer of my arrival
    d. None of the above

18. Which is the best way to punctuate the underlined portion in sentence 2?
    a. They had, as it were, an extent
    b. They had, as it were an extent
    c. They had as it were, an extent
    d. None of the above

19. Which of the following is a synonym for the underlined word in sentence 3?
    a. Think of
    b. Act on
    c. Desire
    d. None of the above

20. Which edit should be made in sentence 4?
    a. Change *out-of-doors* to *outdoors*
    b. Change *she, she only,* to *her and her only,*
    c. Neither A nor B
    d. Both A and B

21. Which is the best replacement for the underlined word in sentence 5?
    a. Humorous
    b. Witty
    c. Amusing
    d. Any of the above

22. Which revision would most improve sentence 5?
    a. Change *step by step* to *step-by-step*
    b. Change *room by room* to *room-by-room*
    c. Change *secret by secret* to *secret-by-secret*
    d. Change *our to our* to *us*
    e. All of the above

23. Based on context clues, what is the most likely meaning of the underlined word in sentence 6?
    a. A design element of the tower
    b. The color of the tower
    c. The shape of the tower
    d. None of the above

24. Which is the best way to separate sentence 6 into two sentences?
    a. Young as she was, I was struck, throughout our little tour, with her confidence and courage with the way, in empty chambers and dull corridors, on crooked staircases that made me pause and even on the summit of an old machicolated square tower that made me dizzy. Her morning music, her disposition to tell me so many more things than she asked, rang out and led me on.
    b. Young as she was, I was struck, throughout our little tour, with her confidence and courage with the way her morning music, her disposition to tell me so many more things than she asked, rang out and led me on. This occurred to me while in empty chambers and dull corridors, and on crooked staircases that made me pause and even on the summit of an old machicolated square tower that made me dizzy.
    c. Young as she was, I was struck, throughout our little tour, with her confidence and courage with the way, in empty chambers and dull corridors, on crooked staircases that made me pause. And even on the summit of an old machicolated square tower that made me dizzy, her morning music, her disposition to tell me so many more things than she asked, rang out and led me on.
    d. Young as she was, I was struck, throughout our little tour. With her confidence and courage with the way, in empty chambers and dull corridors, on crooked staircases that

made me pause and even on the summit of an old machicolated square tower that made me dizzy, her morning music, her disposition to tell me so many more things than she asked, rang out and led me on.

Questions 25-32 are based on the short passage below:

One is always impressed profoundly by the expression of a sense of bulk, vastness, or mass in form (1). There is a feeling of being lifted out of one's puny self to something bigger and more stable (2). It is this splendid feeling of bigness in Michael Angelo's figures that are so satisfying (3). One cannot come away from the contemplation of that wonderful ceiling of his in the Vatican without the sense of having experienced something of a larger life than one had known before (4). Never has the dignity of man reached so high an expression in paint, a height that has been the despair of all who have since tried to follow that lonely master (5). In landscape also this expression of largeness is fine: one likes to feel the weight and mass of the ground, the vastness of the sky and sea, the bulk of a mountain (6).

On the other hand one is charmed also by the expression of lightness (7). This may be noted in much of the work of Botticelli and the Italians of the fifteenth century (8). Botticelli's figures seldom have any weight; they drift about as if walking on air, giving a delightful feeling of otherworldliness (9). The hands of the Madonna that hold the Child might be holding flowers for any sense of support they express (10). It is I think on this sense of lightness that a great deal of the exquisite charm of Botticelli's drawing depends (11).

The feathery lightness of clouds and of draperies blown by the wind is always pleasing, and Botticelli nearly always has a light wind passing through his draperies to give them this sense (12).

25. Which of the following is the best version of the underlined portion in sentence 1?
    a. Always one is profoundly impressed by
    b. One is always impressed profoundly by
    c. Always is one profoundly impressed by
    d. Onc is always profoundly impressed by

26. Which of the following is not a synonym of the underlined word in sentence 2?
    a. Scrawny
    b. Tiny
    c. Feeble
    d. Brawny

27. Which word is not a synonym for the underlined word in sentence 3?
    a. Grand
    b. Superb
    c. Marvelous
    d. Satisfactory

127

28. Which edit should be made in sentence 3?
   a. Change *are* to *is*
   b. Remove the apostrophe in *Angelo's*
   c. Neither A nor B
   d. Both A and B

29. Which revision would most improve sentence 6?
   a. Add *and* before *the bulk of a mountain*
   b. Remove the colon after *fine*
   c. Both A and B
   d. Neither A nor B

30. Which is the best way to punctuate the underlined portion in sentence 7?
   a. On the other hand one is charmed, also by
   b. On the other hand, one is charmed also by
   c. On the other hand, one is charmed, also by
   d. None of the above

31. Which is the best way to punctuate the underlined portion in sentence 11?
   a. It is, I think, on this sense
   b. It is I think on this sense
   c. It is, I think on this sense
   d. It is I think, on this sense

32. Which of the following is the best way to rewrite sentence 12 for increased clarity?
   a. The feathery lightness of clouds and draperies blown by the wind is always pleasing, and Botticelli nearly always has a light wind passing through his draperies to give them this sense.
   b. The feathery lightness of clouds and draperies blown by the wind, of which Botticelli nearly always has, is always pleasing.
   c. Botticelli nearly always has a light wind passing through his draperies to give them the effect of feathery lightness of clouds and draperies blown by the wind is always pleasing.
   d. None of the above

Questions 33-40 are based on the short passage below:

Gregory of Tours informs us, that when Frédégonde, wife of Chilpéric, gave the hand of her daughter Rigouthe to the son of the Gothic king, fifty chariots were required to carry away all the valuable <u>objects which</u> composed the princess's dower (1). A strange family scene, related by the same historian, gives us an idea of the private habits of the court of that terrible queen of the Franks (2). "The mother and daughter had frequent <u>quarrels,</u> which sometimes ended in the most violent encounters." (3) Frédégonde said one day to <u>Rigouthe "Why</u> do you continually trouble me? (4) Here are the goods of your <u>father, take</u> them and do as you like with them." (5) And <u>conducting</u> her to a room where she locked up her treasures, she opened a large box filled with valuables (6). After having pulled out a great number of <u>jewels which</u> she gave to her daughter, she said, "I am tired; put your own hands in the box, and take what you find." (7) Rigouthe bent down to reach the objects placed at the bottom of the <u>box; upon which Frédégonde immediately lowered the lid on her daughter, and</u> pressed upon it with so much force that the eyes began to start out of the princess's head (8). A maid began <u>screaming, "Help! my mistress</u> is being murdered by her mother!" and Rigouthe was saved from an untimely end." (9) It is further related that this was only one of the minor crimes attributed by history to Frédégonde *the Terrible*, who always carried a dagger or poison about with her (10).

33. Which is the best way to punctuate the underlined portion in sentence 1?
    a. objects, which
    b. objects that
    c. Neither A nor B
    d. Either A or B

34. Which of the following is a synonym for the underlined word in sentence 3?
    a. Arguments
    b. Disagreements
    c. Disputes
    d. All of the above

35. Which is the best way to punctuate the underlined portion in sentence 4?
    a. Rigouthe, "Why
    b. Rigouthe Why
    c. Rigouthe, Why
    d. Rigouthe "Why

36. Which is the best way to punctuate the underlined portion in sentence 5?
    a. father. Take
    b. father; take
    c. Neither A nor B
    d. Either A or B

37. Which word is not a synonym for the underlined word in sentence 6?
    a. Leading
    b. Directing
    c. Guiding
    d. None of the above

38. Which is the best way to punctuate the underlined portion in sentence 7?
    a. jewels, which
    b. jewels; which
    c. jewels which
    d. None of the above

39. Which is the best way to punctuate the underlined portion in sentence 8?
    a. box; upon which <u>Frédégonde</u> immediately lowered the lid on her daughter, and
    b. box, upon which <u>Frédégonde</u> immediately lowered the lid on her daughter and
    c. box upon which <u>Frédégonde</u> immediately lowered the lid on her daughter and
    d. box, upon which <u>Frédégonde</u> immediately lowered the lid on her daughter, and

40. Which is the best way to punctuate the underlined portion in sentence 9?
   a. screaming "Help! my mistress
   b. screaming, "Help! my mistress
   c. screaming Help! my mistress
   d. screaming, Help! my mistress

Use the prompt below to answer Question 41.

41. Write an essay in 25 minutes by answering the question from your perspective. Be sure to provide evidence.

   • *In The Dispossessed, published in 1974, groundbreaking science fiction author Ursula K. LeGuin wrote, "You can't crush ideas by suppressing them. You can only crush them by ignoring them."*

   Is it possible to get rid of an idea?

Practice Test 2—Answers

Mathematics

Percent/Part/Whole, Percent

1. **c.**
   $Value_{2000}$ = Original price * (1-.6) → 2500 = .4P = 2500 → P = 6250.

2. **b.**
   Amount = $P(1 + r)^t$ = 500 * 1.05^3 = \$578.81.

3. **e.**
   Final value = $75000(1 - .1)^2$ = 73507.

4. **b.**
   If the original price of the dress was x, then the discounted price would be 0.8x. To increase the price from .8x to x, the percent increase would be (x - .8x)/.8x * 100 = 25%.

5. **a.**
   Let the original price of the car be x. After the 30% increase, the price is 1.3x.

   After discounting the increased price by 30%, it now is .7 * 1.3x = .91x. Therefore, the ratio of the final price to the original price = .91x : x.

Mean, Median, Mode

1. **c.**
   To find the median, we first have to put the list in order:

   27, 28, 29, 30, 35, 37, 41, 43, 44, 45, 46, 50.

   The middle two scores are 37 and 41, and their average is 39.

2. **e. None of the above**
   The mean is just the total score/number of scores → 90 +… + 94)/10 → 79.9.

   The median is the score located in the middle. The middle of the set of the numbers is between 84 and 79. The average of these two scores is 81.5.

   The mode is the number that occurs the most: 78.

3. **a.**
   Multiply each t-shirt price with the number sold; add them together and divide by the total number of shirts sold.

   So Average Price = (4.50 * 8 + 13.25 * 12 + 15.50 * 4)/(8 + 12 + 4) → \$10.71.

Exponents and Roots

1. **c.**
$(a^2*a^{54}+a^{56}+ (a^{58}/a^2))/a^4 = (a^{54+2}+a^{56}+a^{58-2})a^{-4} = 3a^{56-4} = 3a^{52}$.

2. **d.**
9^m is the same as 3^{2m}.

So $3^{2m} = 3^{-1/n}$ → $2m = -1/n$ → $mn = -.5$.

3. **e.**
$2^a * 4^a$ can be re-written as $2^a * (2^2)^a$.

$32 = 2^5$.

Therefore, $2^{(a+2a)} = 2^5$ → $3a = 5$ → $a = 5/3$.

Algebraic Equations

1. **b.**
Use FOIL:

$(3x - 4)(6 - 2x) = 3x * 6 - 4 * 6 + 3x * (-2x) - 4 * (-2x) = 18x - 24 - 6x^2 + 8x = -6x^2 + 26x - 24$.

2. **e.**
Since $6n + m$ is divisible by 3 and 5, the new number that we get after adding a value will be divisible by 3 and 5 only if the value that we add is divisible by 3 and 5. The only number that will work from the given choices is 60.

3. **e.**
We are told $x^3/5 = x/5$ → $x^3 = x$. The possible values are -1, 0, and 1. We are told that x is negative.

So $x = -1$.

4. **e.**
This problem can be done by elimination. We know that m is in the thousands, which means $x * 10^3$; and n is in the hundreds, which is $y * 10^2$. The answer will be $z * 10^5$, or 6 places in total, so we can eliminate **a)**, **c)**, and **d)**. Also we see that m ends in 8 and n ends in 5, so the answer has to end in 0 ($8 * 5 = 40$), which eliminates **b)**.

5. **c.**
The ball has a speed of 30 miles per hour. 30 miles per 60 minutes = .5 mile per minute; 2 minutes and 35 seconds = 2 minutes; and 35/60 minutes = 2.58 minutes.

The ball travels .5 * 2.58 = 1.29 miles.

6. **d.**
$30(\sqrt{40} - \sqrt{60}) = 30\sqrt{4 (10 - 15)} = 60(\sqrt{10} - \sqrt{15})$.

7. **c.**

Multiply the numerator and the denominator by $\left(\sqrt{40} + \sqrt{60}\right)$.

So $\dfrac{30}{\left(\sqrt{40}-\sqrt{60}\right)} * \left[\dfrac{\left(\sqrt{40}+\sqrt{60}\right)}{\left(\sqrt{40}+\sqrt{60}\right)}\right] =$
$30\left(\sqrt{40} + \sqrt{60}\right)/\left(\sqrt{40} - \sqrt{60}\right)^2$.

$-3\left(\sqrt{10} + \sqrt{15}\right)$.

8. **b.**

Find all the prime numbers that multiply to give the numbers.

For 2, prime factor is 2; for 3, prime factor is 3; for 4, prime factors are 2, 2; and for 5, prime factor is 5. Note the maximum times of occurrence of each prime and multiply these to find the least common multiple.

The LCM is 2 * 2 * 3 * 5 = 60.

9. **a.**

One pen sells for $12, so on the sale of a pen, the profit is 12 - 6 = 6.

In order to make $60, we need to sell 10 pens.

Inequalities, Literal Equations, Polynomials, and Binomials

1. **a.**

Solve by substitution.

If $a = b + 3$, and $3b = 5a + 6$, then $3b = 5(b+3) + 6$.

If $3b - 5b - 15 = 6$, then $-2b = 21$. Therefore, $b = -10.5$.

Now use substitution to find a.

$a = b + 3$. So $a = -10.5 + 3$. Therefore, $a = -7.5$.

Solve the equation, $3a - 2b$.

$3(-7.5) - 2(-10.5) = -1.5$.

2. **c.**

If the roots are a and b, then $a + b = 8$ and $a - b = 2$.

Add the equations. $2a = 10 \rightarrow a = 5 \rightarrow b = 3$.

The factors are $(x - 5)(x - 3)$, and the equation is $x^2 - 8x + 15$.

3. **d.**

From the equation $3x + y = 5$, we get $y = 5 - 3x$. Substitute into the other equation. $3x + 2(5 - 3x) = 7$ → $3x + 10 - 6x = 7$ → $x = 1$. This value into either of the equations gives us $y = 2$.

4. **a.**

$4x + 5y = 41$, and $x + y = 9$, where x and y are the number of tickets sold.

From equation 2: $x = 9 - y$.

From equation 1: $4(9 - y) + 5y = 41$ → $36 + y = 41$ → $y = 5$.

5. **a.**

b is the number of boys, and g is the number of girls. So $b + g = 40$, and $2b + 4g = 140$.

To do the problem, use the substitution method. Plug $(g = 40 - b)$ into $(2b + 4g = 140)$.

$2b + 4(40 - b) = 140$ → $b = 10$.

Slope and Distance to Midpoint

1. **b.**

Find the values of the y coordinate for different values of the x coordinate (example, [-3, +3]). We get the following chart:

x	y
-3	-23
-2	-8
-1	1
0	4
1	1
2	-8
3	-23

From these values, we see the graph is symmetrical to the y axis.

2. **a.**

Distance $s = \sqrt{(x_2 - x_1)^2 + (y_2 - y_1)^2}$ → $s = \sqrt{(9 - 3)^2 + (20 - 12)^2} = \sqrt{36 + 64} = 10$.

3. **b.**

$y = mx + b$; m is the slope and b is the y intercept.

Calculate m for line AB using the given points $(0, -3)$ and $(-2, 1)$. $m = (-3 - 1)/(0 - (-2)) = -2$. The y intercept is -3 (from point set given), so $y = -2x - 3$.

4. **b.**

First, find the slope, $(y_2 - y_1)/(x_2 - x_1)$ → slope $= (12 - 2)/(6 - 1) = 2$.

Next, use the slope and a point to find the value of b.

In the standard line equation, $y = mx + b$, use the point $(6, 12)$ to get $12 = (2 * 6) + b$ → $b = 0$.

The equation of the line is $y = 2x$.

5. **e.**
The midpoint is at $(x_1 + x_2)/2, (y_1 + y_2)/2 = (1,7)$.

6. **c.**
Slope $= (y_2 - y_1)/(x_2 - x_1) = 3$. Plug one of the coordinates into $y = mx + b$ to find the value of b.

$1 = 3(1) + b$ → $b = -2$.

The equation of the line is $y = 3x - 2$.

7. **c.**
Calculate the slope of each line. Slope of line A $= 4/3$; and slope of line B $= y - 6$.

The slopes of the line have to be the same for the lines to be parallel.

$4/3 = y - 6$ → $4 = 3y - 18$ → $y = 22/3$.

8. **c.**
The slope of line A $= \frac{1}{2}$; and the slope of line B $= (y - 7)/2$.

The product of the slopes has to equal -1.

$(1/2)[(y - 7)/2] = -1$ → $(y - 7)/4 = -1$ → $y = 3$.

9. **c.**
Slope$_b = (5 - 1)/(10 - 8) = 2$. The slope of line A is -1/2.

To find the intercept of line B, use $y = mx + b$.

$5 = (2)(10) + b$, so $b = -7$. Equation of line B is $y = 2x - 7$.

Find intersect x, using the given y coordinate. $14 = 2x - 7$; $x = 10.5$.

Find the intercept of line A using the coordinates of intersection.

$14 = (-1/2)(10.5) + b$. $b = 19\frac{1}{4}$.

The equation of line A is $y = -(1/2)x + 19\frac{1}{4}$.

Absolute Value Equations

1. **d.**
   The lowest value of $f(x)$ can be 0, since $f(x)$ is equal to a squared value, but, for $f(x) = 0$, x must equal -2. That is outside the domain of x. The least value of $f(x) = 4$.

2. **b.**
   $x^2 - 9$ can be factored into $(x + 3)$ and $(x - 3)$.

   $[(x + 3)(x - 3)]/(x - 3) = x + 3$.

3. **d.**
   If the roots are 5 and -8, then the factors are $(x - 5)(x + 8)$. Multiply the factors to get the equation.

   $x^2 + 3x - 40$.

4. **d.**
   After 5 weeks, the number of ants = $100 + 32$, or 132.

5. **d.**
   Expand the equation:

   $[16x^2 + 40x + 25 - 40x - 25]^{1/2} + 3|x| - 14 = 0$.

   $(16x^2)^{1/2} + 3|x| - 14 = 0$.

   $4x + 3|x| - 14 = 0$.

   $3|x| = 14 - 4x$.

   $|x| = \dfrac{14}{3} - \dfrac{4x}{3}$ $\qquad x = \dfrac{14}{3} - \dfrac{4x}{3} = 2 \qquad x = -\dfrac{14}{3} - \dfrac{4x}{3} = 14$.

6. **a.**
   $x = 4$ and $y = 5$, $|x + y| = 9$.

   $x = -4$ and $y = 5$, $|x + y| = 1$.

   $x = 4$ and $y = -5$, $|x + y| = 1$.

   $x = -4$ and $y = -5$, $|x + y| = 9$.

7. **d.**
   The absolute value of x can be at least a 0, and is otherwise positive regardless of the value of x.

   $y \geq 0$.

Geometry

1. **b.**
   Perimeter of a rectangle = $2(l + w)$. Width = $5 - x$; and length = $4(5 - x)$.

   Perimeter = $2(l * w) = 30$ → $2(20 - 4x + 5 - x) = 30$ → $-10x = -20$ → $x = 2$.

2. **d.**
   Side AC = 5, and side BC = 4. The Pythagorean triple is 3:4:5, so side AB = 3.

   Because the other triangle is similar, the ratio of all sides is constant. AB:AB = 3:24. The ratio factor is 8.

   AC of the larger triangle = $5 * 8 = 40$.

3. **d.**
   The area of a circle = πr^2.

   If the diameter is doubled, then the radius is also doubled.

   The new area = $\pi * (2r)^2 = 4 * \pi * r^2$. The area increases four times.

4. **a.**
   $\angle P = 55^0$. $\angle Q = 90^0$. $\angle R = 180 - (55 + 90) = 35^0$, and $\angle A = 180 - 35 = 145^0$.

Fundamental Counting Principle, Permutations, Combinations

1. **c.**
   $\#Choices_{today} = {}^5P_2 = 5!/(5 - 2)! = 5 * 4 = 20$.

   $\#Choices_{tomorrow} = {}^3P_2 = 3!/1! = 6$.

   $\#Choices_{day3} = 1$.

   The total number of permutations = $20 * 6 * 1 = 120$.

2. **c.**
   This is a combinations problem. The order of the numbers is not relevant.

   $^{10}n_5 = 10!/5!(10 - 5)! = 10 * 9 * 8 * 7 * 6/5 * 4 * 3 * 2 * 1 = 252$.

3. **e.**
   There are 3 ways to choose an appetizer, 6 ways to choose a beverage, and 3 ways to choose an entrée. The total number of choices = $3 * 6 * 3 = 54$.

4. **d.**
   $^{10}C_3 = 10!/(3!(10 - 3)!) = 10!/(3! * 7!) = 10 * 9 * 8/3 * 2 * 1 = 120$.

5. b.
$${}^{10}P_4 = 10!/3!(10 - 3)! = 10 * 9 * 8/3 * 2 * 1 = 120$$

Ratios, Proportions, Rate of Change

1. e.
If $n/m = .5$, then $n = .5m$, or $n = \frac{1}{2}$ of m.

2. c.
The total number of fruit = 26.

The probability of picking a pear = 5:26.

The probability of picking an apple = 10:25.

The probability of picking a pear and an apple = 5:26 * 10:25 = 50:650 = 1:13.

3. b.
The total number of fruit = 12.

The probability of picking a fig = 2;12.

The probability of picking an apple = 3;11.

The probability of picking a fig and an apple = 2;12 * 3;11 = 6;132 = .045.

Round up to .05.

4. d.
The overall rate for x workers = the number of toys/ the number of days, p/c. The number of toys one worker makes per day (rate) = p/cx. If q is the number of toys y workers make, and the rates are equal, then the number of toys made = the rate x.

The number of days * the number of workers gives us $q = p/cx$ (dy), so:

$q = pdy/cx$.

5. d.
The distance travelled = (35/1)(13) = 455 miles.

Reading Comprehension

1. c.
2. d.
3. a.
4. a.
5. a.
6. b.

7. d.
8. a.
9. c.
10. a.
11. c.
12. b.
13. a.
14. b.
15. a.
16. a.
17. c.
18. b.
19. a.
20. a.
21. c.
22. b.
23. a.
24. c.
25. a.
26. a.
27. c.
28. c.
29. b.
30. b.
31. c.
32. d.
33. c.
34. a.
35. b.
36. d.
37. c.
38. b.
39. b.
40. c.

Writing

1. c.
2. a.
3. b.
4. c.
5. a.
6. c.
7. d.
8. a.
9. d.
10. b.
11. b.

12. a.
13. d.
14. a.
15. d.
16. d.
17. c.
18. a.
19. a.
20. d.
21. d.
22. e.
23. a.
24. b.
25. d.
26. d.
27. d.
28. a.
29. a.
30. b.
31. a.
32. b.
33. d.
34. d.
35. a.
36. d.
37. d.
38. a.
39. b.
40. b.
41. **Score of 5+:**

The suppression of ideas has been attempted over and over throughout history by different oppressive regimes. This theme has been explored as well in literature, through such dystopian works as 1984 and Fahrenheit 454. But these histories and stories always play out the same way: eventually, the repressed idea bubbles to the surface and triumphs. Ursula K. LeGuin acknowledged this by saying that ideas can be crushed not by suppression, but by omission.

In Aldous Huxley's novel Brave New World, the world government maintains order not by governing people strictly and policing their ideas, but by distracting them. Consumption is the highest value of the society. When an outsider ot the society comes in and questions it, he is exiled—not to punish him, but to remove his influence from society. The government of the dystopia has learned that the best way to maintain control is to keep citizens unaware of other, outside ideas. This theme resonates with a modern audience more than other, more authoritarian tales of dystopia because in our society, we are less controlled than we are influenced and persuaded.

Repressing ideas through harsh authoritarian rule has proven time and again to be ultimately fruitless. For example, in Soviet Russia during the 1920s and 1930s, Josef Stalin attempted to purge his society of all religious belief. This was done through suppression: discriminatory laws were enacted, members of the clergy were executed, and the religious citizenry were terrified. While these measures drastically crippled religious institutions, they were ineffective at completely eliminating the idea of religion. Beliefs and traditions were passed down in communities clandestinely throughout the repressive rule of Stalin. After the fall of the Soviet Union, it became clear that religion had survived all along.

We see throughout literature and history that ignoring ideas and distracting people from them is generally more effective than to attempt to stamp an idea out through means of suppression. Authoritarian rule, in fact, can do the opposite: by dramatizing and calling attention to an idea in the name of condemning it, a regime might actually strengthen that idea.

Score of 3-4:

We have seen different governments try to crush out ideas throughout history. However, they are never actually successful in doing so. An idea can be ignored or suppressed, but it will never really go away. This is illustrated in the survival of religion in the Soviet Union.

In Soviet Russia during the 1920s and 1930s, Josef Stalin attempted to purge the society of all religious belief. This was done through suppression: discriminatory laws, execution of the clergy, and use of terror. While this harmed religious institutions, they were ineffective at crushing the idea of religion. Beliefs and traditions were passed down in communities secretly throughout the rule of Stalin. After the fall of the Soviet Union, it became clear that religion had survived all along.

The same kind of thing happened with apartheid law in South Africa. Even though there were laws against black Africans and white Africans using the same facilities, the idea caught fire, especially because of an international outcry against the law.

We see throughout history that suppressing ideas does not crush them. Authoritarian rule, in fact, can do the opposite: by calling attention to an idea in the name of condemning it, a regime might actually strengthen that idea.

Score of 2 or Less:

It is not possible to crush out an idea by ignoring it or by suppressing it. All throughout history, whenever anyone has tried to do this, they might be temporarily successful but the idea will always survive or come back. For example in the Soviet Union religion was suppressed. People were not allowed to practice their religion. But after the government fell, religion still existed – people had held on to their ideas during the time of suppression.